Reading Comprehension:
Teacher Resource
and
Student Activities
Grade 6

BY
DOROTHY NELSON

COPYRIGHT © 2001 Mark Twain Media, Inc.

ISBN 1-58037-153-1

Printing No. CD-1374

Mark Twain Media, Inc., Publishers
Distributed by Carson-Dellosa Publishing Company, Inc.

Table of Contents

Table of Contents

Table of Contents

Introduction: *Finding Their Passion*

How many times have you lamented, "How do I motivate my students? They just don't seem to care. I can't get them engaged. They just won't do the work." **The missing piece of the puzzle is passion**. Our students often do not see the relevancy in what we ask them to do. Most of the work done in our classrooms is seen as "school work," not "life work" or "*my* work."

How can the teacher help students discover what is important to them? With many of your students, it takes just a little time and opportunity to find out their interests in horses or fishing or collecting bean bag toys. However, there are other reticent young people who struggle to find their passions. To help students discover and expand their interests, we must create a literate environment in which each student can share in a community ownership.

This book is offered as a scaffolding for reading instruction. First, we need to know our students as readers. This is the teacher's first task and will provide critical information to inform our instruction. We also need to recognize the power of conversation and dialog about our reading. We need to engage students in the reading process before, during, and after reading. Next, we need to teach our students the explicit strategies for learning vocabulary. Students need to make connections between new words and words that are already familiar to them. We also need to teach students how to apply explicit strategies when reading different genres of fiction and nonfiction. Finally, we need to teach students how to deal with test questions. Whether it is for required district or state testing, students need to be prepared for the format of test taking and the thinking that is required to answer specific kinds of questions.

All teachers are reading teachers. We must *strategically plan* to teach explicit reading strategies to support our students' academic success.

Reproducible student pages are included throughout the book. Additional copies of student pages that may be used frequently are included in the back of the book in the appendix.

Chapter 1: Establishing a Reading Environment: *Checklist for a Print-Rich Environment*

My vision of the ideal classroom that would attract readers looks like a cozy bookstore in which a person would love to browse. In order to provide enough titles to entice a student to read, a classroom book collection should include 300 to 1,000 books. Reflect on the following checklist for a print-rich environment and use it to create your own "bookstore classroom" that invites your students in to browse, read, inquire, and learn.

_____ Books are on display around the room with availability for checkout.

_____ Fiction books by favorite authors are available.

_____ Books by specific genre are available and labeled (suspense, horror, historical fiction, etc.)

_____ Nonfiction books are available that correspond with science, social studies, math, and other subjects being studied and/or researched.

_____ Traditional reference book collection is available with dictionaries, thesauruses, almanacs, atlases, English handbooks, etc.

_____ Other reference books for specific subjects are available (hunting and fishing licenses, motorcycle catalogue, consumer information on various products, pamphlets on drug abuse, etc.). *These items are often donated by parents and students.*

_____ Magazines and newspapers are made available. *These items are often donated by parents and students.*

_____ A poetry nook is available where a certain poet or types of poems are highlighted each month. Students can respond to the poetry in a "Poetry Nook Guest Book" that is an integral part of the poetry nook.

_____ A shared reading area with books and audiotapes is available to inspire students to read a book they are interested in but that may be too difficult to read on their own.

_____ A computer with a variety of educational software is available.

_____ Many opportunities to self-select reading are available.

Name: _____ Date: _____

Chapter 1: Establishing a Reading Environment: *Create a Classroom Map*

Directions: Draw a detailed map of your classroom. Be sure to label all the features of your room and the directions of each wall. Draw a star at each location where reading takes place. Draw a plus sign at locations where a reading center could be set up if your classroom does not already have one.

Chapter 1: Sharing: *Keeping a Writer's Notebook*

Teacher Directions: Plan strategically for activities in which students and teacher can think about and share what they know, enjoy, and wonder about.

Student Directions:

Keep a Writer's Notebook.

- Record in it daily.

- Record questions.

- Record things you enjoy doing.

- Record things you know a lot about.

- Record things you wonder about and want to know more about.

- Record favorite books, authors, magazines, and so on.

- Record field trip notes.

- Record memories.

- Record observations about people, yourself, nature,

  the world, something you have read, and so on.

- Create illustrations.

- Include photographs.

- Include examples of good openings.

- Include examples of good closings.

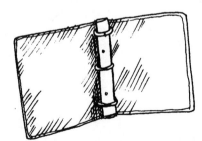

- Include examples of figurative language.

Chapter 1: Sharing: *Share Your Passion*

Teacher Directions: Model for students with your personal list on an overhead, flip chart, or white board.

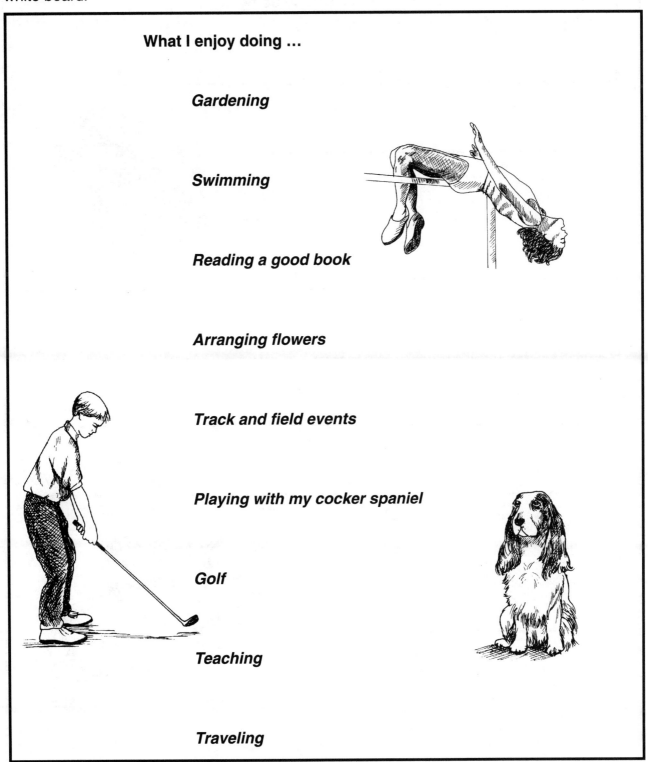

What I enjoy doing ...

Gardening

Swimming

Reading a good book

Arranging flowers

Track and field events

Playing with my cocker spaniel

Golf

Teaching

Traveling

Name:_____ Date:_____

Chapter 1: Sharing: *Share Your Passion*

Student Directions: List as many things as you can that you enjoy doing.

What I enjoy doing ...

1. _____

2. _____

3. _____

4. _____

5. _____

6. _____

7. _____

8. _____

9. _____

10. _____

Chapter 1: Sharing: *Share Your Passion*

Teacher Directions: Model for students with your personal list on overhead, flip chart, or white board.

I know a lot about ...

Writing

Dogs

U. S. government

Trees

Italy

Door County, Wisconsin

Maya Angelou

William Shakespeare

Polar bears

Poetry

Acting

Reading

Collecting polar bear toys

Name:_____ Date:_____

Chapter 1: Sharing: *Share Your Passion*

Student Directions: List as many topics as you can that you know a lot about.

I know a lot about …

1. _____

2. _____

3. _____

4. _____

5. _____

6. _____

7. _____

8. _____

9. _____

10. _____

Chapter 1: Sharing: *Share Your Passion*

Teacher Directions: Model for students with your personal list on overhead, flip chart, or white board.

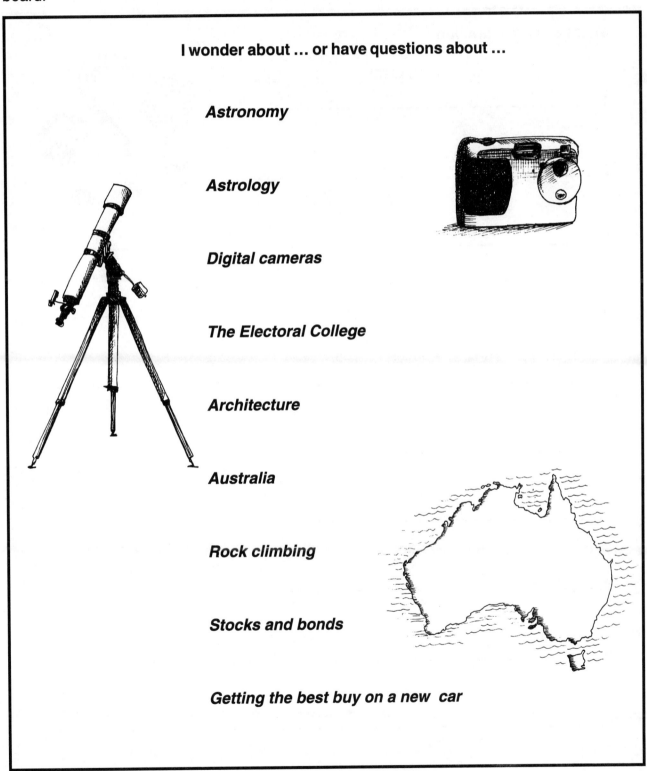

I wonder about ... or have questions about ...

Astronomy

Astrology

Digital cameras

The Electoral College

Architecture

Australia

Rock climbing

Stocks and bonds

Getting the best buy on a new car

Name: _____ Date: _____

Chapter 1: Sharing: *Share Your Passion*

Student Directions: List as many topics as you can that you would like to learn more about.

What I want to learn about ...

1. _____

2. _____

3. _____

4. _____

5. _____

6. _____

7. _____

8. _____

9. _____

10. _____

Chapter 1: Developing a Reader's Identity: *Reading Attitude Survey*

Students need time for and a structure for thinking, observing, and talking about their reading. Providing strategic activities to teach students how to think critically, to observe closely, and to dialogue clearly is important.

1. **Reading Attitude Surveys**
   (Routinely, teachers should stop and ask students to think about and talk about their reading behavior.)

Reading Attitude Survey A

What makes me want to read?

(Sample answers)

Learning how to put something together

Choosing my own book

Comic books

When my friend likes a book

What makes me not want to read?

(Sample answers)

Reading with a partner

Assignments in the social studies book

Reading boring books

When I have to write about it

***An adaptation of this survey is to ask students to give a reason why.

Name: _____ Date: _____

Chapter 1: Developing a Reader's Identity: *Reading Attitude Survey*

Reading Attitude Survey B

Student Directions: Place a check mark in the column that describes how often you do the following things.

How often do you/are you …	Often	Sometimes	Never
• Write or talk with others about your reading.			
• Feel confident in your reading.			
• Notice what you are thinking as you are reading.			
• Know when you don't understand your reading.			
• Change your reading behavior when you don't understand something you are reading.			
• Notice when you are distracted while reading.			
• Able to go back and find specific facts in the text after reading.			
• Continue to read even when confused or bored.			
• Able to read longer texts over a longer period of time.			

These surveys can be done individually, in small groups, or with the whole group as a shared writing or a focus lesson. The teacher may just want to ask one of the questions as a timed "quick write."

Chapter 1: Developing a Reader's Identity: *Reading Attitude Survey*

Reading Attitude Survey C

Teacher Directions: Quick writes are a great way to compel students to think about their reading. They can be done in one to ten minutes. Hint: Use a timer. Do not wait for all students to be finished. Use the information as quick feedback to you and/or the beginning for a small or whole group discussion.

Quick Write 1

Please respond to the following in the allotted time:

> *Describe what you do when you are reading and you come to a word or concept that you don't know.*

Quick Write 2

Please respond to the following in the allotted time:

> *Describe how you go about selecting a book to read from the classroom, school libraries, or stores.*

Quick Write 3

Please respond to the following in the allotted time:

> *Describe what you do before you begin reading.*

Chapter 1: Developing a Reader's Identity: *Reading Attitude Survey*

Reading Attitude Survey C (continued)

Quick Write 4

Please respond to the following in the allotted time:

Describe what you do or what you are thinking during your reading.

Quick Write 5

Please respond to the following in the allotted time:

Describe what you do or what you are thinking after you read.

14

Name: _____ Date: _____

Chapter 1: Developing a Reader's Identity: *Reading Attitude Survey*

Reading Attitude Survey D

Student Directions: Answer the following questions about reading.

1. How many books do you have of your own?

   _____

2. How many books have you read this month?

   _____

3. What kinds of books do you like to read?

   _____

4. Who is your favorite author?

   _____

5. What magazines or newspapers do you like to read?

   _____

6. How did you learn to read?

   _____

7. When you are reading and you come to something you don't know, what do you do?

   _____

8. What makes a good reader?

   _____

9. Do you think you are a good reader? Why or why not?

   _____

10. Why do you think reading well is important?

    _____

Name:_____   Date:_____

Chapter 1: Developing a Reader's Identity: *Reading Attitude Survey*

Reading Attitude Survey E

Student Directions: Highlight the statements that are true about you.

1. I talk to my family or friends about a good book I have read.

2. I like to reread a favorite book.

3. I read books at home that are not part of schoolwork.

4. I read books by the same author.

5. I go to the library to check out a book.

6. I can understand what I am assigned to read in school.

7. I feel proud about how I read.

8. I know reading helps me learn about many subjects.

9. I enjoy reading aloud in class.

10. I like to listen to a book being read aloud.

11. I like to read.

Name: _____ Date: _____

Chapter 1: Developing a Reader's Identity: *Student Self-Assessment of Reading*

Reading Attitude Survey F

Student Directions: Place a check in the box that describes how well or how often you do the following things.

I Can …	I Try	Sometimes	Always
Remember things I already know.			
Make predictions about what will come next.			
Summarize what I read.			
Sound out words I don't know.			
Give people detailed facts about what I have read.			
Make pictures in my mind as I read.			
Figure out what the author means from different parts of my reading.			
Try reading words I don't know.			
Use expression when I read aloud.			
Guess the meaning of a word because it looks like another word I know.			
Break words into syllables.			
Ask questions to myself or to the author as I read.			

Chapter 1: Developing a Reader's Identity: *Prompts to Guide Peer Discussion*

Learning is social. If students are to become strategic, confident readers who enjoy reading, they must be able to talk about their reading. Providing many opportunities each day for students to discuss their reading and their comprehension of what they've read is critical.

Prompts to Guide Peer Discussion

- What did you like about your book?

- What did you learn?

- How did it make you feel?

- Were there any difficult parts to understand?

- What parts of the story were of special interest to you?

- When you read, did it make you think of other people, places, and/or experiences you've had?

- What was one of your favorite parts? Why?

- What do you know that you didn't know before you read your book?

- Were there any parts of the book that you would have changed if you had been the author?

- What did you think the author did especially well?

- Would you recommend the book to other classmates? Why or why not?

Name: _____ Date: _____

Chapter 1: Developing a Reader's Identity: *Keeping a Writer's Notebook*

Teacher Directions: A wonderful way for students to continue to identify themselves as readers is to have them, at the same time, identify themselves as writers. Have students keep a writer's notebook in which they keep a running list of things they write and the purposes for which they write.

Student Directions: Record what you write and the reasons you write in your writer's notebook.

What I Write	
What I Write for Myself and Others	**What I Write for My Teacher(s)**

Chapter 1: Questioning: *Question-Answer Relationships*

Questions play a critical role in the learning process. Questioning is an integral part of reading and learning from a text. Unfortunately, usually teachers are the only ones who determine the important questions, and students are expected to answer. Following are some activities for guiding students to independent questioning that will lead them to independent learning.

Teaching students effective questioning will help them take more of an analytical approach to their reading. The Question-Answer Relationship (QAR) strategy developed by Raphael (1982, 1984, 1986) helps students to categorize different types of questions for their learning.

Four Types of Question-Answer Relationships

Right There
The answer is explicitly stated in the text.

Think and Search
The answer can be found in several places in the text.

Author and You
The answer is not in the text. The reader must use the author's information and his or her own background knowledge to figure out an answer.

On My Own
The answer is not in the text. The reader must use his or her personal experience to answer the question.

How do you teach students to identify the different types of questions?

1st   The teacher will model these four kinds of questions in literature and with content area reading.

2nd   The teacher provides many opportunities for students to identify and categorize the different types of questions found in their textbooks or in class discussion.

3rd   Examples of the different types of questions are displayed in the room and added to as other questions are analyzed.

4th   Gradually, teachers will need to do less prompting as their students become more actively engaged in their reading and in generating their own questions.

Name: _____ Date: _____

Chapter 1: Questioning: *Question-Answer Relationships*

Teacher Directions: In a read-to or independent reading, students will hear or read chunks of a text and then identify the types of questions.

Example

Ludwig van Beethoven

Music was Ludwig van Beethoven's whole life. He started piano lessons before he was even four years old. He was so small that he had to stand on the piano bench so he could reach the keys. His father was a stern man who would rap his son's knuckles whenever he made a mistake. Young Beethoven would often cry as he stood in front of the piano. As he got older, his alcoholic father would wake Ludwig in the middle of the night to show him off to his drinking friends whom he brought home with him from the taverns.

By the time he was twelve years old, Beethoven was publishing music and earning money to support his family when his father could no longer take care of them. Although Beethoven had a very difficult childhood, he eventually became known as the greatest pianist of his time. His music was so beautiful that sometimes his listeners wept.

His extraordinary talent and playful personality attracted many friends. Unfortunately, his moodiness and sarcasm made it hard for him to keep friends. He once insulted a very influential prince by telling him, "There are and there will be thousands of princes. There is only one Beethoven."

21

Name: _____ Date: _____

Chapter 1: Questioning: *Teacher Model/Guided Student Practice*

Teacher Model: Read each question and help students determine what type of question it is.

1. What was Beethoven's extraordinary talent?

   Right There   Think and Search   Author and You   On My Own

2. How do we know that Beethoven had a difficult childhood?

   Right There   Think and Search   Author and You   On My Own

3. How did Beethoven's childhood affect his life?

   Right There   Think and Search   Author and You   On My Own

4. Should parents pressure very young children to excel in sports, music, or other academic areas? Why or why not?

   Right There   Think and Search   Author and You   On My Own

Guided Student Practice: Develop a question from each of the four categories and provide the answer.

1. Right There Question: _____

   Answer: _____

2. Think and Search Question: _____

   Answer: _____

3. Author and You Question: _____

   Answer: _____

4. On My Own Question: _____

   Answer: _____

Chapter 1: Questioning: *Fertilizing the Classroom for Asking Those Compelling Questions*

All teachers can create a classroom environment that invites and challenges students to ask significant questions. Instead of interrogating students, we must provide opportunities for the students to ask the questions and do the inquiry. That will in turn produce active and engaged learning.

TRY:

- **Clarification Session**

  At some point during the day, ask students to write down a sincere question about any content being studied in the classroom. They can write it on a sticky note, an index card, or a slip of paper. Select those questions that need clarification and have a group problem-solving session. This not only clears up confusion for the individual asking the question, but also for the ten others who didn't ask.

- **Who Knows? Question Game**

  During the week, ask students to record any "I wonder …" questions and place them in a specified Question Box. Their questions may be about content being studied in class or any other subject they are curious about. Set aside a 15–20 minute time slot for students to pull out question cards and ask the questions for the group to answer. Any questions that cannot be answered by anyone in the room, including the teacher, become invitations for individual inquiry. If a student later finds the answer, he or she can share it with the class during the next Who Knows? Question Game.

- **Today's News**

  Provide students with access to varied magazines and newspapers. During independent reading time, encourage students to include the reading of some periodicals. Sometime during the week, schedule a class discussion on real issues, events, and people in the news. Record the various questions that evolve from the discussion. **Discourage students from asking "yes" and "no" questions.**

Chapter 1: Questioning: *Fertilizing the Classroom for Asking Those Compelling Questions (continued)*

• Code the Text

Provide students with sticky notes to keep track of the questions they have as they read. They can either code it with just a question mark or sometimes write the question out so they do not forget. If they have their own copy of the text, they can highlight or code it in the margin.

• Charting the Journey

When students begin a theme study or a unit of study in science or social studies, create a community chart that tracks the journey of inquiry. Start with the **BIG Question** and begin to chart the key questions that need to be answered. Over time, add new questions to the chart that surface as you continue the research.

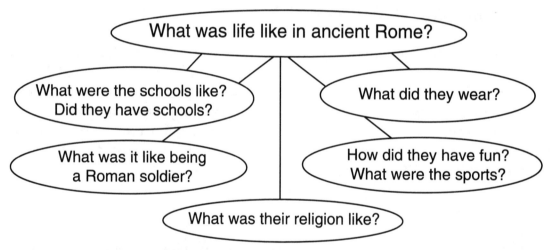

• K-W-L Charts (Ogle 1986)

It is important for students to ask *significant* questions that will lead to in-depth inquiry. Teach students that they cannot ask good questions about something they know nothing about! The familiar K-W-L chart can be a very effective tool to help students build on their prior knowledge, but it can also be misused. First, it must be modeled for the whole class. When it is used for independent inquiry, the students must determine the items in the "What I want to know …" column from the items in the "What I know …" column. The items in the "What I learned …" column should clearly reflect answers to "What I want to know."

What I Know …	What I Want to Know …	What I Learned …

Chapter 2: Engaging Students in the Reading Process: *Teaching Reading Strategies*

We have several serious concerns about our students' reading. We are concerned that our students do not read, that they say they do not like to read, or that when they do read they "can't remember" the main ideas. We are concerned about the students who do excellent "word call" but cannot carry meaning. We are concerned about their lack of comprehension and ability to make connections. But mostly, we are concerned that they do not find joy in their reading. The truth is, they will never find joy in reading until they are in control of their reading. They will not enjoy reading until the confusion is gone. They will not enjoy reading until it makes sense.

Students must be taught to be strategic readers. Teachers must **explicitly plan and strategically teach the strategies for reading**. Teachers must do ongoing assessment and plan to teach specific **content**. With this content, specific **skills, strategies, and concepts** are taught using "strategically planned **activities**." It is this "strategic planning" of instruction that will help students to gain control in their reading.

Reading instruction should take place all day across the curriculum. We have made a mistake in scheduling our reading and writing as separate parts of the day. Reading quality fiction is an important part of reading instruction, but it is equally important to know how to read informational texts. In fact, our students often struggle more with nonfiction text than with novels or short stories.

One of the best ways to engage students in reading is to have an abundance of nonfiction (informational) texts, as well as quality fiction books in your classroom. Young people are drawn to texts about animals, people, places, and activities outside of the school scene. It is a natural way to teach students more about their reading and to expand their knowledge.

Reading strategies can be taught in all texts when the teacher "strategically plans" those activities that will teach those reading strategies.

Chapter 2: Engaging Students in the Reading Process:
Specific Reading Comprehension Strategies

What are the specific reading comprehension strategies?

Good readers use these strategies independently, automatically, and quickly.

1. **Predict.**

2. **Make connections.**

3. **Determine the most important ideas and themes.**

4. **Clarify and ask questions of themselves and the author.**

5. **Use prior knowledge.**

6. **Summarize.**

7. **Create visual images.**

8. **Use fix-up strategies.**

*** *Teachers need to use authentic and challenging texts (high-quality literature and well-written nonfiction) to help their students move from novice to proficient readers.*

Chapter 2: Using Strategies Before, During, and After Reading: *Strategies of Proficient Readers*

Teacher Directions: Use these suggestions to teach specific reading strategies.

♦ **Proficient readers think about their own thinking during reading.**
  - model
  - think aloud as you read
  - use specific reading terminology with students
  - expect students to use specific reading terminology

♦ **Proficient readers know when they do comprehend and when they do not comprehend.**
  - help students chunk information and focus their attention on chunks of text at a time
  - encourage students to use graphic organizers
  - work collaboratively

♦ **Proficient readers can identify their purposes for reading in different types of texts.**
  - model
  - think aloud as you read different types of text
  - provide opportunities for students to read and research a variety of texts
  - invite students to write for a variety of purposes

♦ **Proficient readers know when and why the meaning of a text is unclear to them.**
  - model
  - think aloud
  - teach students to generate their own questions
  - provide opportunities for students to dialogue about their reading

♦ **Proficient readers use a variety of strategies to solve comprehension problems.**
  - model
  - think aloud
  - teach specific strategies of what to do when they don't know the meaning of a word
  - teach specific strategies of what to do when they don't understand something they have read
  - provide opportunities for students to share with the class what strategies they use

Chapter 2: Using Strategies Before, During, and After Reading: *Strategies of Proficient Readers (cont.)*

Explicit Strategies to Teach

♦ **How to make predictions and activate prior knowledge before, during, and after reading a text**

Proficient readers will make connections of newly learned information with their own lives, the world, and other texts read.

♦ **How to determine the most important ideas and themes in a text**

Proficient readers draw conclusions about important ideas and exclude unimportant details from memory.

♦ **How to ask questions of themselves and the authors**

Proficient readers use their questions to clarify their reading.

♦ **How to make inferences from texts they are reading**

Proficient readers use their prior knowledge and the information from the text to draw conclusions to form interpretations of the text.

♦ **How to retell what they have read**

Proficient readers can identify the most important information and articulate that into a summary.

♦ **How to create visual images from the texts they are reading before, during, and after reading**

Proficient readers will use these images to enhance their comprehension of the text.

♦ **How to use a variety of fix-up strategies to self-correct when they do not comprehend**

Proficient readers select appropriate fix-up strategies to problem-solve during their reading.

Chapter 2: Planning Activities to Teach Reading Strategies:
How to "Strategically Plan" to Teach Reading Strategies

Teacher Directions: Use the following key questions as a guide for planning instruction.

How do I know what my students know and are able to do?

    Assessment:

      How do I determine the content I will teach?

      Curriculum:

What are the skills, strategies, and concepts that I need to teach with the content?

    Reading Strategies:

What activities will be most effective to teach those strategies?

    Activities:

    How do I assess to find out if they can use the strategy?

    Assessment:

Chapter 2: Planning Activities to Teach Reading Strategies:
How to "Strategically Plan" to Teach Reading Strategies

Example

How do I know what my students know and are able to do?

Assessment:
Pre-test
Class discussion
Written response
Anecdotal observations
Other

How do I determine the content I will teach?

Curriculum: (Science curriculum - "The Universe")
Resources:
Science text
Variety of nonfiction trade books and reference books
Related periodicals
Video and computer software
Guest speaker

What are the skills, strategies, and concepts that I need to teach with the content?

Reading Strategies:
To use prior knowledge
To predict
To determine main ideas
To clarify
To question
To summarize

Chapter 2: Planning Activities to Teach Reading Strategies: *How to "Strategically Plan" to Teach Reading Strategies*

Example (continued)

What activities will be most effective to teach those strategies?

> **Activities:**
>> Sneak Preview Vocabulary
>>
>> Shared Reading
>>
>> Paired Reading
>>
>> Independent Reading/Coding the Text
>>
>> Quick Write

How do I assess to find out if they can use the strategy?

> Post-test
>
> Written response
>
> Oral presentation
>
> Multimedia presentation
>
> Debate
>
> Brochure or newsletter
>
> A mural or model for exhibition
>
> A slide show put to music

*** *In strategically planning for instruction, it is always important to plan for multiple intelligences. This literally helps to "level the playing field" for everyone's success.*

Chapter 2: *Planning Activities to Teach Reading Strategies: Reader's Workshop*

Strategy Lesson Plan 1

It is important to begin strategy instruction with texts that are close to the students' own experiences. This allows the children to learn new ways to think about their reading. When children have heard and read an extensive array of narrative and expository texts, they stretch and begin to make connections between books and their lives. They can then begin to make connections from what they read to the world. Now they are ready to think about and read about more challenging issues and themes.

Reader's Workshop

Focus Lesson - 5–15 minutes.

> During this time, the teacher works with the whole group to introduce, model, teach, and/or record the students' thinking and understanding of specific skills and reading strategies.

Workshop - 25–40 minutes.

> During this time, the teacher does guided instruction with small groups of students for literature study, reciprocal teaching, or special needs groups.

Sharing - 5–10 minutes.

> During this time, students share with the whole group their literature responses, questions, observations, or favorite passages.

Chapter 2: Planning Activities to Teach Reading Strategies: *Independent Reading*

Strategy Lesson Plan 2

Independent Reading

Choice - 15–20 minutes.

Provide daily time for silent sustained reading. Students have the choice of what they want to read; however, it is important to encourage students to read varied genre.

Purpose

Give students a specific purpose for their reading. This should be strategically planned to reinforce reading strategy instruction.

Examples:

- Ask students to mark a passage in their reading that creates a visual image for them.
- Ask students to be prepared to share a one- or two-sentence summary.
- Ask students to jot down two of the best descriptive words that the author used.
- Ask students to be prepared to predict what will happen next.
- Ask students to be prepared to share why they selected their reading material.

Independent Reading

During this time, the teacher can hold reading conferences with students. These conferences can be used to teach or reinforce a specific reading strategy, listen to a student read, check for comprehension with a re-tell, or find out more about the student's attitude and habits of reading.

Sharing - 5–7 minutes.

Allow students to share with the whole group or with partners what they were asked to think about while they read.

Name: _____ Date: _____

Chapter 2: Planning Activities to Teach Reading Strategies: *Using Predictions to Make Connections*

Strategy Lesson Plan 3

Student Directions: As you read, pay close attention to the parts of the text when you find yourself making **a prediction**. Using the form below, jot down the first and last word of the passage or identify the picture that helped you make a prediction. Then write down your prediction. When you have finished your reading, go back and check to see if your predictions actually happened. Then write down what really happened.

Passage or Picture: _____

Prediction: _____

_____

Was your prediction right? _____ If not, what did happen? _____

_____

Passage or Picture: _____

Prediction: _____

_____

Was your prediction right? _____ If not, what did happen? _____

_____

Passage or Picture: _____

Prediction: _____

_____

Was your prediction right? _____ If not, what did happen? _____

_____

Passage or Picture: _____

Prediction: _____

_____

Was your prediction right? _____ If not, what did happen? _____

_____

Name: _____ Date: _____

Chapter 2: Planning Activities to Teach Reading Strategies: *Making Connections to Your Own Life*

Strategy Lesson Plan 4

Student Directions: As you read, pay close attention to the parts of the text when you find yourself making **a connection to your own life**. Using the form below, jot down the first and last word of the passage or identify the picture where you made the connection to your life. Then write down your connection.

Passage or Picture: _____

_____

Connection to My Life: _____

_____

_____

_____

_____

Passage or Picture: _____

_____

Connection to My Life: _____

_____

_____

_____

_____

Name: _____ Date: _____

Chapter 2: Planning Activities to Teach Reading Strategies: *Making Connections to Another Text*

Strategy Lesson Plan 5

Student Directions: As you read, pay close attention to the parts of the text when you find yourself making **a connection to another text that you have read**. Using the form below, jot down the first and last word of the passage or identify the picture where you made the connection to another text. Then write down your connection.

Passage or Picture: _____

_____

Connection to Another Text I've Read: _____

_____

_____

_____

_____

_____

Passage or Picture: _____

_____

Connection to Another Text I've Read: _____

_____

_____

_____

_____

Name: _____   Date: _____

Chapter 2: Planning Activities to Teach Reading Strategies: *Making Connections to the World*

Strategy Lesson Plan 6

Student Directions: As you read, pay close attention to the parts of the text when you find yourself making **a connection to other knowledge you have about the world.** Using the form below, jot down the first and last word of the passage or identify the picture where you made the connection to other knowledge. Then write down your connection.

Passage or Picture: _____

_____

Connection to the World: _____

_____

_____

_____

_____

_____

Passage or Picture: _____

_____

Connection to the World: _____

_____

_____

_____

_____

_____

Name:_____ Date:_____

Chapter 2: Planning Activities to Teach Reading Strategies:
Determining the Most Important Ideas and Themes

Strategy Lesson Plan 7

Student Directions: As you read, record the main ideas and themes in the selection.

Mapping Main Ideas As You Read		
Page #	**One Main Idea**	**One or Two Details**

Chapter 2: *Planning Activities to Teach Reading Strategies: Determining the Most Important Ideas and Themes*

Strategy Lesson Plan 8

Teacher Directions: This activity can be done as a whole class with partners or as an assigned activity for two or more students. Select a given "chunk" of reading material (two to three pages in length) for students to read. Divide the class into groups of two partners, A and B, and ask them to follow the directions. **This needs to be modeled several times before students will do it independently.**

"Keep An Eye On My Reading"

Partner A -

- Select a paragraph or two to read orally as your partner follows along.
- Predict what you think will be the main idea of the paragraph(s).
- Read in a "six-inch voice" to your partner.
- When finished, turn the book over, and summarize in one or two sentences what you just read.

Partner B -

- Select the next paragraph or two to read orally as your partner follows along.
- Predict what you think will be the main idea of the paragraph(s).
- Read in a "six-inch voice" to your partner.
- When finished, turn the book over, and summarize in one or two sentences what you just read.

Partners A and B -

- Select the next paragraph or two to read **silently**.
- Predict together what you think will be in the next chunk of reading.
- When finished, turn the books over, and **Partner A** summarizes in one or two sentences what you just read.
- **Partner A asks Partner B** if he or she wants to add anything to **Partner A's** summary.

Chapter 2: *Planning Activities to Teach Reading Strategies: Determining the Most Important Ideas and Themes*

Strategy Lesson Plan 8 (continued)

Partners A and B -

- Select the next paragraph or two to read **silently**.
- Predict together what you think will be in the next chunk of reading.
- When finished, turn the books over, and **Partner B** summarizes in one or two sentences what you just read.
- **Partner B asks Partner A** if he or she wants to add anything to **Partner B's** summary.

Partners A and B -

- Finish reading the assignment independently.
- When finished, **write a two-question quiz for your partner on only the last chunk of reading.**

  Be sure both questions are Right There questions.

  Be sure you know the answers.

  Remember, the questions cannot be **Yes or No** questions.
- Give your partner no more than five minutes to complete the quiz.
- Check your partner's quiz. Tell him or her how he or she did.
- Complete your partner's quiz and get the results from him or her.
- Turn both quizzes in to your teacher.

Name: _____   Date: _____

Chapter 2: *Planning Activities to Teach Reading Strategies*: *Determining the Most Important Ideas and Themes*

Strategy Lesson Plan 8 (continued)

"Keep An Eye On My Reading"
QUIZ

Title: _____

Pages read for quiz: _____

Student taking the quiz: _____

Question 1: _____

_____

Answer: _____

_____

Question 2: _____

_____

Answer: _____

_____

Student giving the quiz: _____

Student Check

Question 1:   **Correct** _____ **Incomplete** _____ **Incorrect** _____

Comment: _____

_____

Question 2:   **Correct** _____ **Incomplete** _____ **Incorrect** _____

Comment: _____

_____

Chapter 2: Planning Activities to Teach Reading Strategies: *Clarifying and Asking Questions of Themselves and the Author*

Strategy Lesson Plan 9

Word Wall Scramble
(Parts of Speech)

Teacher Directions:

1. Establish the routine of posting unknown words or concepts that have been discussed for clarity from the students' reading in all content areas.

2. Students determine which words they feel are valuable words to know and be able to use. Students can also determine which words can be retired from the word wall. *(Students may choose to have a topic word wall that addresses vocabulary and concepts for a particular unit of study in social studies or science.)*

3. Words on the word wall can be organized in any way that meets the needs of the class. The most common way to organize is alphabetically.

4. Periodically have a WORD WALL SCRAMBLE. Students can work in pairs, small groups, or individually. The SCRAMBLE can be done at the word wall or on separate sheets of poster paper. Students are asked to make connections. For example, students may be asked to organize the words according to parts of speech. They could work in small groups and be assigned a specific part of speech. Nouns could be written on white cards, verbs on blue, adjectives on yellow, and so on. One group could determine the appropriate adverb for the adjectives.

5. Students present their lists to the group. The class discusses the accuracy of the connections.

Chapter 2: Planning Activities to Teach Reading Strategies: *Clarifying and Asking Questions of Themselves and the Author*

Strategy Lesson Plan 9 (continued)

Word Wall Scramble
(Variations)

Categorize by Theme

1. Students categorize words that can be related to the same theme or concept. This is a wonderful way to teach difficult concepts as well as vocabulary. For example, the class may be studying the Civil War and the theme of freedom. They may have selected the following words that relate to the concept of freedom:

independence	**courage**	**sacrifice**	**constitutional**
democracy	**choice**	**valor**	**government**
perseverance			

2. Students may add other words that they feel are also related to the concept.

Antonym or Synonym

1. Students select ten words to find antonyms for.

2. They then select ten words to find synonyms for.

Chapter 2: Planning Activities to Teach Reading Strategies: *Using Prior Knowledge*

Strategy Lesson Plan 10

Word Wall Detective

Teacher Directions:

1. Select 10 to 20 words from a new piece of literature you will be studying. Put them on an overhead, flip chart, or a white board.

2. Include words or phrases that give clues to characters, setting, and possible problems in the story.

3. As a whole-group activity, discuss the following questions.

   • Who do you think will be characters in the story? Why do you think that?
   • Where do you think the story takes place? When? Why do you think that?
   • What do you think the problems will be in the story? Why do you think that?

   *** *(This activity can be done with nonfiction as well.)*

Example: (Taken from a story about Sir Gawain and the Green Knight)

warriors	**dishonored**	**Yuletide festival**
Round Table	**waning winter light**	**fair lady**
dark moors	**drawbridge**	**unlaced his helmet**
flattery	**honor prevailed**	**failed through cowardice**

Name: _____ Date: _____

Chapter 2: *Planning Activities to Teach Reading Strategies: Summarizing*

Strategy Lesson Plan 11

Teacher Directions: This activity teaches the strategy of summarizing as "thinking as the student reads," not just at the end of the reading.

Think About It As You Read

Student Directions:

1. As you read the selection, keep an eye out for the **most important words or phrases.** The words could be names, details, or actions.

2. Jot these most important words on your key word list.

3. Use these words to help you write a summary of what you have read.

Name _____

Reading Assignment _____

Key Words

_____

_____

_____

Summary

_____

_____

_____

_____

Underline the key words that you included.

45

Name: _____ Date: _____

Chapter 2: Planning Activities to Teach Reading Strategies: *Creating Visual Images*

Strategy Lesson Plan 12

Teacher Directions: Teach students to watch for words and phrases that authors use to bring about strong visual images. These are descriptions that make us see it, hear it, and/or feel it.

Look to the Author

Name _____

Book _____

Student Directions: Select five key words or phrases that create strong sensory images. These can be metaphors, similes, comparisons, alliterative language, and so forth.

1. _____

2. _____

3. _____

4. _____

5. _____

Use one or more of your selections above to write a description. Try to write a description that makes a connection to your life.

> **Example:** "…flushed crimson with embarrassment."

I flushed crimson with embarrassment when I tripped in the lunchroom. It seemed as if the whole world was laughing at me.

Chapter 3: Teaching Vocabulary: *Introduction*

For 25 years, I was adamant about my students increasing their vocabulary. Also for 25 years, I was frustrated with the results of my instruction of vocabulary. What was I doing wrong? How could I help my students **effectively and accurately** use the vocabulary that I taught *or thought I taught?* It was often an exercise in futility. Even with the students who would get "A's" on the vocabulary tests, I saw no carry-over into their own speaking and writing.

We know that knowledge of vocabulary directly impacts reading comprehension. So what do we need to do differently in order to get different results? The answer lies in teaching *concepts rather than definitions.* When I gave my weekly vocabulary tests, I varied the type of questions among multiple choice, matching, writing definition, and using words in a sentence. Whenever I changed the wording of the definition, my students could not make the connection, because they did not understand the larger concept of the word. The question now becomes, "How do we teach concepts?"

If we truly want to increase vocabulary and improve reading comprehension, we must think differently about our instruction. This will mean that we must abandon some traditional practices that are not resulting in success for most of our students. The best teachers and the best learners are reflective. Reflect on the following aspects of vocabulary instruction.

Use the strategy lesson plans in this chapter as specific strategies for teaching vocabulary. Blank, reproducible student forms from this chapter are available in the appendix at the back of this book.

Chapter 3: Teaching Vocabulary: *Changing Our Thinking About Vocabulary Instruction*

- **Read aloud to your students every day.**

- Increase time for reading as part of your daily instruction.

- Use varied genres of high-quality texts.

- Increase your nonfiction selections in the classroom.

- Avoid the assignment of looking up definitions to words as the primary source for word knowledge. *(Knowing how to use the dictionary as a resource is very important, but it is not the best way to **learn and understand** how to use new vocabulary successfully in written and oral language.)*

- Avoid assigning students to independently use words in sentences before they understand the concept of the word.

- Use concrete examples whenever possible.

- Provide multiple opportunities for students to **use and hear** the vocabulary words in the classroom. *(One of the best teaching strategies is to use those "BIG WORDS" in your instruction whenever appropriate.)*

- Plan strategically for activities that require students to connect new words to words and concepts they already know.

- Stop assigning students a list of vocabulary words to look up **before** reading a text. Some students may be reluctant to read a text that they now perceive may be too difficult. You may want to pre-teach a concept, historical reference, or other reference that is needed to comprehend the text. However, pre-teaching a long list of vocabulary will make your students dependent on YOU to do the problem-solving when it comes to encountering "BIG WORDS."

Chapter 3: Teaching Vocabulary: *Changing Our Thinking About Vocabulary Instruction (cont.)*

- **Abandon the belief that students need to have all words defined in order to comprehend a text.** *(Your students need to know that good readers come across many words that need clarification. Many of your most struggling readers believe they are poor readers because they do not know certain words when they read.)*

- Emphasize the word or concept that is most important for comprehending the text. Avoid the confusion of superficially covering the definitions of several vocabulary words before reading.

- Provide explicit instruction of word analysis (root words, prefixes, suffixes, and so on) for independent word learning.

- Teach your students how to determine meaning in context. This will require that you teach students that good readers know when they do not understand and that there are often clues within the context of their reading. Sometimes they need **to stop** when they do not understand and reread or read ahead.

- Provide many opportunities for students to discuss **inferences, meanings of idiomatic phrases, and figurative language.**

- Remember that "LEARNING IS SOCIAL." Provide students with many opportunities to use the new vocabulary and concepts in their own speaking.

- **Use those "BIG WORDS" as part of your vocabulary in the classroom.** (*Don't be afraid to "talk UP" to students. You will discover your students using the same words that you use.*)

- ## HAVE FUN WITH WORDS.

Chapter 3: Teaching Vocabulary: *Activating Prior Knowledge*

Strategy Lesson Plan 1

Teacher Directions: Select 2-3 key vocabulary words or concepts to assess prior knowledge. Remember that these words and concepts should be significant to comprehending a particular text. Ask students to think about what they know about those words.

Example

DO YOU KNOW THESE WORDS?

If you think you know or you are sure of the meaning, please write your definition in the appropriate column.

1. auctioneer

2. gangplank

3. docilely

No clue	I've seen it or heard it	I think I know	Yes, I've got it
1.	1. ✔	1.	1.
2. ✔	2.	2.	2.
3.	3.	3.	3.

Chapter 3: Teaching Vocabulary: *Word-Context-Connection*

Strategy Lesson Plan 2

Teacher Directions: To make students more conscious of using context to determine the meaning of a word, follow the steps below:

1. Ask students to work in groups of three or four. Each student is to identify one word from their reading that he or she does not know. *(Each student should select a different word.)*

2. Each student individually records his or her thinking on the Context-Connection graphic organizer.

3. After completing the graphic organizer, students share their thinking with their small group. *(Give students only 1–2 minutes to share their thinking.)*

(Note: This is a rich activity that allows students, in a very short time, to practice the strategies needed to clarify, to understand the concept of a new word, and to use the word in writing and speaking.)

Chapter 3: Teaching Vocabulary: *Word-Context-Connection*

Strategy Lesson Plan 2 (Example)

Student Directions: Identify one word from your reading that you do not know. Then complete the graphic organizer below about the word.

Context-Connection

Write the word in context: *"I want a refund immediately," the man said belligerently.*

- **Circle the word needing clarification.**

- **Read the surrounding sentences.**

Identify two possible definitions:

1. *meanly*
2. *angrily*

Look up the definition in the dictionary:
    (adverb) warlike; ready to fight

Use the word in a different context: *My brother belligerently stomped into our room.*

Make a personal connection: *I was belligerent when my mom said I couldn't go to the mall with Amy.*

Chapter 3: Teaching Vocabulary: *Think-Analyze-Connect*

Strategy Lesson Plan 3

Teacher Directions: To find out what students already know about certain concepts or the words that relate to it, follow the steps below:

1. Ask students to brainstorm independently all the words they can think of that relate to a word or concept. *Set a timer for no more than 3–5 minutes to complete this activity.*

2. Ask students to add to their list by thinking about ...
   • Synonyms.
   • Antonyms.
   • People, places, or things that might be described using this word or a form of this word.
   • Events or situations in which this word might be used.

3. Ask students to work in pairs to compare lists and put their words in labeled categories. The students may identify words that just do not fit in a certain category. *(These words should be listed separately.)*

4. Options after categorizing words:
   • Papers may be turned in to the teacher for assessment.
   • Students may present to the whole class.
   • Teacher and students may complete a shared writing in which the teacher scribes all of the categories identified by the class with examples under each category.

Chapter 3: Teaching Vocabulary: *Think-Analyze-Connect*

Strategy Lesson Plan 3 (continued)

***Example:* An Adaptation for Literature**

Identified word or concept: intolerable

(If this is a key word needed to understand an important problem in the story and you also think this is an important vocabulary word, you may want to vary the activity if the students have no knowledge of the word.)

1. Ask students if they can identify what part of speech it is. You may have students who will be able to tell you that it is an adjective because it ends in "able."

2. Ask students if they can identify anything else about the word.

3. Give students a brief definition:
    Intolerable describes something that cannot be endured any longer; unbearable or too painful to be endured.

4. Ask students to add to their list by thinking about ...
    • Synonyms.
    • Antonyms.
    • People, places, or things that might be described using this word or a form of this word.
    • Events or situations in which this word might be used.

    | severe | bearable | rudeness | persecution of Jews |
    | impossible | possible | heat of the desert | cheating on a test |

5. Ask students to work in pairs to write a paragraph about the reading so far.
    (The students are asked to include the word "intolerable" in their summary.)

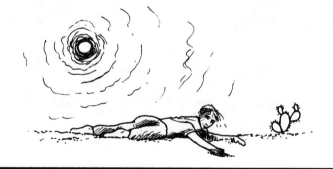

Chapter 3: Teaching Vocabulary: *Think-Analyze-Connect*

Strategy Lesson Plan 3 (continued)

***Example:* An Adaptation for Social Studies**

Content: Social Studies, "The History of the American Indians"

Identified word or concept: Archaeology and American Indians

1. Ask students to brainstorm independently everything they know about "archaeology and how archaeologists helped us learn about the American Indians." *Set a timer for no more than 3–5 minutes to complete this activity. On an overhead or flip chart, the teacher should also brainstorm along with the students. This will ensure that certain words like "carbon-14 dating" and "dendrochronology" are included.*

2. Ask students to work in pairs to discuss their "before views" about the archaeology and the history of the American Indians.

3. Ask each student to write one question that they have about the subject. The teacher will scribe the questions and post them in the classroom for ongoing clarification during the study of the history of American Indians.

4. After the unit of study, ask students to work in small groups to create a cognitive map of what they know about the American Indians. *The teacher supplies each group with a large sheet of poster paper to demonstrate what they know about the subject in writings as well as in symbols and pictures.*

5. Students present their group maps to the class.

6. Use any objective or subjective assessment to evaluate learning.

Name:_____ Date:_____

Chapter 3: Teaching Vocabulary: *Using Story Vocabulary to Retell*

Strategy Lesson Plan 4

Teacher Directions: To help students comprehend what they read as well as to build vocabulary, keep a running list of vocabulary words posted that students have generated during the story about characters, setting, main idea, most important events, problems, and solutions. Several times during the literature study, ask students to use the word list to do a variety of activities.

KEY WORD STRATEGY

Student Directions: Using the running list of vocabulary discussed during this novel, fill in the following blanks with appropriate words or phrases.

Two words or phrases about a main idea

_____, _____

Two words or phrases about a character

_____, _____

Two words or phrases about a setting

_____, _____

Two words or phrases about an important event

_____, _____

Two words or phrases about a problem

_____, _____

Two words or phrases about the solution

_____, _____

Name: _____ Date: _____

Chapter 3: Teaching Vocabulary: *Using Story Vocabulary to Make Connections*

Strategy Lesson Plan 5

Teacher Directions: Students will select one or more characters from their reading and keep a running list of words and phrases used to describe that character. These words can come from the text itself or other connections that have been made through literature circle discussion. Ask students to make connections to themselves, other people they know, or other characters in books they have read. *(This activity can be adapted to identifying an event, problem, or solution that they can connect to themselves, someone else they know, the world, or other books.)*

That reminds me of ...

Student Directions: Select a character from your reading. Using the running list of words and phrases to describe this character, identify four words or phrases that you believe are the most significant in describing that character. Select any one of those traits to compare to yourself, someone you know, or another character in a book. Give a specific explanation why you made that connection.

Character _____

Traits _____

_____

_____

_____

That reminds me of myself because _____

_____

_____

_____

Name: _____　Date: _____

Chapter 3: Teaching Vocabulary: *Using Story Vocabulary to Make Connections*

Strategy Lesson Plan 5 (continued)

That reminds me of _____ because _____

_____

_____

That reminds me of another character, _____, in the book

_____

because _____

_____

_____

Chapter 3: Teaching Vocabulary: *How to "Attack" Words*

Strategy Lesson Plan 6

Teacher Directions: Explicitly teach students the different ways to attack words they do not know that they encounter in their reading.

1. In a whole class focus lesson, ask students to share with the class what they do when they read and encounter words and concepts they do not know. *(Teacher scribes the list on a flip chart paper to be posted in the room or has copies made for students to keep in their reader's notebooks. It is important that the teacher add any key strategies that students miss.)*

2. Routinely stop and have students review those strategies in small groups, one-on-one conferences, or in whole-class discussion.

3. On occasion, have students reflect on their reading of a particular assignment. Ask them to do a "quick write" in 3–5 minutes, explaining what strategies they used during their reading.

4. Ask students to share with a partner.

5. Ask students to turn in quick writes for a "QUICK" assessment.

Chapter 3: Teaching Vocabulary: *Word Attack Skills*

Strategy Lesson Plan 6 (continued)

(A sample list of context strategies)

WORD ATTACK SKILLS

1. Think about what makes sense in the sentence.

2. Read the other words around the word.

3. Reread the sentence.

4. Reread the paragraph.

5. Skip it if you do not need to know the word to understand the text.

6. Sound out the word.

7. Keep reading to see if there are key words that might clarify the meaning.

8. Look at any pictures or captions.

9. Look the word up in the dictionary.

10. Ask someone.

Example

   "Sandy had a dilemma. She could not decide if she should jump or risk getting attacked by the bear."

Definition: dilemma - *(noun) any situation requiring a choice between unpleasant alternatives.*

Name: _____   Date: _____

Chapter 3: Teaching Vocabulary: *Looking at Words by "Degrees"*

Strategy Lesson Plan 7

Teacher Directions: To help students increase their vocabularies and thereby improve their reading comprehension, have them examine the slight nuances in words that often determine meaning in context. Identify two vocabulary words that have opposite meanings. Have students generate words or phrases that describe the varied degrees between those two words. Students will then work in pairs to decide on the appropriate descending order.

Example

MICROSCOPIC	ALWAYS	ARROGANT	CIVILIZED
minute			
miniature			
tiny			
little			
small			
medium			
average			
large			
huge			
enormous			
colossal			
titanic			
GIGANTIC	**NEVER**	**ASHAMED**	**UNCIVILIZED**

Name: _____ Date: _____

Chapter 3: Teaching Vocabulary: *"Family Matters"*

Strategy Lesson Plan 8

Teacher Directions: To help students use more effective word analysis and thereby improve their reading comprehension, have them examine the varied word forms ("word families") that can be generated from just one word. **Model** several and **discuss meanings.** Post examples in the room or have copies that the students can use as a reference.

Examples:

wire	wires	wired	wiry	wireless
regular	regulate	regularly	regulation	regularity
symbol	symbolic	symbolism	symbolical	
exact	exactly	exacts	exacted	exacting exactness

Have students practice in pairs, small groups, or independently.

Word Families

Student Directions: Generate as many different forms of each word as you can. Each set of words can be thought of as a "word family."

Protect _____

_____

Community _____

_____

Motion _____

_____

Wood _____

_____

Imagine _____

_____

Original _____

_____

Name: _____ Date: _____

Chapter 3: Teaching Vocabulary: *"Family Matters"*

Strategy Lesson Plan 8 (continued)

An adaptation for this activity is to have students generate "word families" of similar meaning.

Student Directions: Generate as many words as you can that have a similar meaning to the main word.

Example 1: **LAUGH**　　　　　*Example 2:* **FRIEND**

giggle　　　　　　　　　　**companion**

snicker　　　　　　　　　　**buddy**

chuckle　　　　　　　　　　**pal**

cackle　　　　　　　　　　**partner**

hoot　　　　　　　　　　**acquaintance**

guffaw　　　　　　　　　　**ally**

　　　　　　　　　　　　　　　　co-worker

　　　　　　　　　　　　　　　　chum

Select two of your favorite words and write a sentence using each one.

1. _____

_____

2. _____

_____

Chapter 3: Teaching Vocabulary: *The Magic of Prefixes and Suffixes*

Strategy Lesson Plan 9

Teacher Directions: The magic of prefixes and suffixes is that just a few letters at the beginning or end of a word can help a student build his or her vocabulary by leaps and bounds. Make sure all students have a list of prefixes and suffixes that they can use as a reference. Strategically plan to have students identify and discuss the meanings of prefixes and suffixes every day. This can be done in many ways.

- During a daily oral language lesson
- In a focused spelling lesson
- During literature study when clarifying words
- During social studies or science when clarifying words
- During a shared reading
- During a one-on-one writing or reading conference

Example:

1. Have students brainstorm other word forms for *realize.*
    realized, realizing, realizes, realization

2. Have students discuss how suffixes change how the word is used.

3. Review the rule that the suffix "tion" makes a word (especially a verb) into a noun.

4. Have students generate other words ending in "tion."
    determination, imagination, defragmentation, separation, combination, etc.

Name: _____ Date: _____

Chapter 3: Teaching Vocabulary: *Idiomatic Interpretation*

Strategy Lesson Plan 10 (Example)

Teacher Directions: Use high-frequency words, as well as examples from students' reading, to teach idiomatic interpretation. The students and teacher will generate a list of idiomatic phrases and discuss the meaning. The students are then asked to work in pairs and write a sentence using three of the five idiomatic expressions listed below.

Fun With Idioms

High-frequency Word: **CHARGE**

Idiomatic Expressions: *(To be generated by students and teacher)*

- To charge something off
- To get a charge out of something
- To be in charge
- To take charge
- To be in charge of someone

Student Directions: Use three of the idioms in sentences that clearly reflect each idiomatic expression.

1.   *The bull charged, and the men scattered.* _____

   _____

2.   *Sara was in charge of preparations for the party.* _____

   _____

3.   *He really got a charge out of riding the thrilling roller coaster.* _____

   _____

4.   _____

   _____

5.   _____

   _____

Use the "Fun With Idioms" activities on the following pages to introduce students to idiomatic expressions. A blank form is provided in the appendix to copy for student use during their own reading.

Name: _____ Date: _____

Chapter 3: Teaching Vocabulary: *Idiomatic Interpretation*

Fun With Idioms

High-frequency Word: **WORTH**

Idiomatic Expressions:

- A bird in the hand is worth two in the bush
- To put in your two cents' worth
- To be worth your salt
- Not worth a hill of beans
- For all it is worth
- To be worth its weight in gold
- To get your money's worth
- An ounce of prevention is worth a pound of cure

Student Directions: Use five of the idioms in sentences that clearly reflect each idiomatic expression.

1. _____

   _____

2. _____

   _____

3. _____

   _____

4. _____

   _____

5. _____

   _____

Name: _____   Date: _____

Chapter 3: Teaching Vocabulary: *Idiomatic Interpretation*

Fun With Idioms

High-frequency Word: **JUMP**

Idiomatic Expressions:

- To jump the gun
- To jump through hoops
- To get the jump on something
- To jump off the deep end
- To get one jump ahead
- To jump down someone's throat
- To jump at the chance

Student Directions: Use five of the idioms in sentences that clearly reflect each idiomatic expression.

1. _____

   _____

2. _____

   _____

3. _____

   _____

4. _____

   _____

5. _____

   _____

Chapter 4: Teaching Genre: *Introduction*

In the last 10 to 15 years, reading and writing instruction has changed dramatically. We have moved from using published basal reading series and workbooks to using literature. A literature-based reading program is the term used to describe a reading program in which students read quality literature in many different themes and genres. In a literature-based reading program, students have choice along the way.

When literature-based reading programs were implemented, the traditional ability level grouping for reading instruction was no longer an option. Teachers organized their reading instruction into reading workshops, literature study groups, and literature circles. These instructional tools relied on the reading instruction to be done as students read and responded to literature. Reading instruction became an interactive, social process.

Unfortunately, without the structure of a basal, many teachers feared that they were not teaching all of the necessary skills and strategies. Most literature study groups had great conversations about books, but reading comprehension was not necessarily improving. More students were enjoying reading, but teachers recognized there must be more explicit teaching of reading strategies and word analysis skills *(see Chapters 2 and 3)*.

It was also a concern that the majority of books that were taught in the literature study groups were fiction. The explicit teaching of how to read expository text was not being addressed. Poetry and fantasy were other genres in which students struggled to comprehend.

This chapter will address the importance of teaching children "how to read" different genres. Remember, we must strategically plan to create a reading environment that contains a variety of genres. Our lesson plans must include the **specific** activities we will use to teach **specific** skills, concepts, and reading strategies. Although there are teachable moments, our teaching is not incidental ... it is planned.

Chapter 4: Teaching Genre: *Fiction*

Reading literature should be a meaning-driven activity that is steered by the reader, not the teacher or textbook. For decades, literature was taught so that students, with close reading, would arrive at the "correct" interpretations of the piece of literature. The role of the student being an active meaning-maker was ignored. We did not teach our students that reading was an exciting journey into making personal connections to their lives, the world, and other texts.

I will never forget when we were studying *Julius Caesar* during my sophomore year in high school. At the end of Act IV, my English teacher stopped and asked us, "Do the ends ever justify illegal or immoral means?" She asked us to write our response and give our reasons for that response. The next day, my English teacher came into the classroom and silently stood before us, grim-faced. Then she slowly stated, "I have never known such a number of immoral students. Yesterday six of you responded that there are times when illegal or immoral means are justified. That is simply wicked, and you should each be ashamed." I was one of the six. I vowed then and there that I would never offer my opinion of a piece of literature unless I knew it matched what the teacher wanted.

As teachers, if we want literature to speak to our students about their lives, we must provide an environment in which they can pursue their own reading and construct their own meaning. At the same time, the teacher needs to have a process with which to teach background knowledge, reading strategies, and skills needed to have purposeful reading. The following pages will outline key components of an interactive reading program.

Chapter 4: Teaching Genre: *The Beginning: What's in It for Me?*

Strategy Lesson Plan 1

Teacher Directions: Use these goals to guide your literature-based reading program.

GOALS:

- Students will have daily opportunities to read, listen to, discuss, and write about what they read.

- Students, as readers, will make meaning of their own using their prior knowledge and experience.

- Student-initiated questions will be an integral part of constructing meaning before, during, and after reading.

- Writing about what they read will enhance student comprehension.

- Students will routinely meet in small groups to discuss their reading.

- The study of literature will be a collaborative experience between teacher and students.

- The teacher will provide rich, literary knowledge and experience as part of the study of literature.

- Thematic connections will be emphasized so that students can make literary connections to diverse texts.

Chapter 4: Teaching Genre: *The Beginning: What's in It for Me?*

Strategy Lesson Plan 1 (continued)

Teacher Directions: Use the following steps to identify the value of reading fiction.

1. Scribe on a flip chart, overhead, "white" board, or blackboard all ideas generated by students to the question, "What is the value of reading literature?"

2. Add any additional components that may be missing.

    Literature is about life. It allows us to get inside the life of another character and to see life through his eyes. Literature helps us learn about feelings, relationships, other places, and other times in history. Literature can make us laugh, cry, be afraid, wonder, get angry, and be inspired to better our own lives. Literature is a way to know ourselves better, to know what we believe, and to know what we should or might do in different situations.

3. Ask students to use any of the generated responses to do a QUICK WRITE to the following question: *(Give students no more than 5–7 minutes.)*

    "How can reading good books and stories help me to be the best I can be?"

71

Name: _____ Date: _____

Chapter 4: Teaching Genre: *Literary Elements of Realistic Fiction*

Strategy Lesson Plan 2

Teacher Directions: Pre-assess to find out what your students know about the following literary components.

Student Directions: Define the following literary components.

1. **Introduction** _____

_____

2. **Setting** _____

_____

3. **Major Characters** _____

_____

4. **Minor Characters** _____

_____

5. **Conflict** _____

_____

6. **Point of View** _____

_____

7. **Plot** _____

_____

8. **Theme** _____

_____

9. **Resolution** _____

_____

10. **Imagery** _____

_____

_____

Name: _____   Date: _____

Chapter 4: *Teaching Genre: Literary Elements of Realistic Fiction*

Strategy Lesson Plan 2 (continued)

Teacher Directions: Pre-assess to find out what your students know about the following literary terms.

Student Directions: Define the following literary terms.

1. **Analogy** _____
   _____

2. **Alliteration** _____
   _____

3. **Atmosphere** _____
   _____

4. **Inference** _____
   _____

5. **Foreshadowing** _____
   _____

6. **Mood** _____
   _____

7. **Simile** _____
   _____

8. **Metaphor** _____
   _____

9. **Symbolism** _____
   _____

10. **Irony** _____
    _____
    _____

analogy SYMBOLISM Atmosphere

Chapter 4: Teaching Genre: *Thematic Variety Within the Genre*

Strategy Lesson Plan 3

Teacher Directions: Select themes that will guide your realistic fiction selections.

Popular themes among adolescent readers:

- **Friendship**   • **Mysteries**

- **Families**   • **Animal Adventures**

- **Survival**   • **Sports**

- **Humor**   • **Growing Up**

  • **Choice and Consequences**

growing up Sports
humor SURVIVAL
animal adventures
families MYSTERIES

Chapter 4: Teaching Genre: *Keeping a Reading Notebook*

Strategy Lesson Plan 4

Teacher Directions: At the beginning of the school year, have students begin to keep a reading notebook in which they respond to a variety of reading. At least once per quarter, have students reflect on themselves as readers by completing a survey. On occasion, post the general results of the class's answers. *(Example: 20 out of 28 students have a favorite author.)*

Think about yourself as a reader and answer the following questions in your reading notebook.

1. What is the title of a book you are currently reading on your own? If you are not reading one now, what is the title of the last book you read?

2. What kinds of literature do you enjoy reading most (mystery, romance, science fiction, sports, horror, short stories, etc.)?

3. Do you have a favorite author? If so, who is it? Why do you like this author's writing?

4. What is the best book you have ever read? Why?

5. How do you feel about what you read at home versus what you read at school? Explain.

Chapter 4: Teaching Genre: *Focus Lesson on Reading Notebooks*

Strategy Lesson Plan 5

Teacher Directions: Include several procedural focus lessons on what makes a quality reading notebook. Give students a copy of the following guidelines.

Guidelines for Keeping a Reading Notebook:

1. Take time during your reading to respond personally to the text. It may be questions; it may be predictions or personal connections. You may want to reflect on a character or event. There may be some description the writer used that impressed you, and you want to be sure to remember it.

2. Sometimes the teacher will ask you to respond to a particular question.

3. There is no assigned length. Sometimes only a few sentences will be enough for your response. At other times, you may write a page or two. The important thing is that you respond every day and that your responses reflect your thoughts and reflections on your reading.

4. Do not summarize what happened in the story. Sometimes I will ask you to respond to a particular question. If you need help, refer to some of these response starters:

   - *I was surprised by ...*
   - *A question I have ...*
   - *I don't understand ...*
   - *That reminds me of ...*
   - *I wonder about ...*
   - *I predict that ...*
   - *I need to clarify ...*
   - *My favorite description or passage was ...*

5. There is no right or wrong response. We each react to a text in our own unique way based on our experiences.

6. Remember that your reading notebook is written to be shared. Your reading notebook is a way for you to record your original ideas, to share your ideas with others, and to add to your ideas.

7 Spelling and grammar are always important. The purpose of writing is to communicate to others. Be sure you write clearly so that your classmates or I can read your entries.

8. Your reading notebook will be graded routinely and randomly for the quality of your response. I will determine a grade based on the frequency and thinking put into your responses. Your responses themselves will not be graded as right or wrong.

Chapter 4: Teaching Genre: *Reading Notebook Response Rubric*

Strategy Lesson Plan 5 (continued)

Teacher Directions: Use the following rubric for grading students' notebook responses. Give students a copy of the rubric so they know what is expected of them.

Reading Notebook Response Rubric

4 points each if student

- Shows awareness of levels of meaning.
- Makes text-to-self, text-to-world, and text-to-text connections.
- Is aware of author's point of view.
- Has used explicit reference to the text.
- Recognizes the author's writing style and its impact on the way the reader feels.

3 points each if student

- Demonstrates the ability to frame questions and predict.
- Response moves beyond a retelling.
- Makes connections.
- Is working to think about the text and understand it.
- Demonstrates some understanding of the characters' motivation.

2 points each if student

- Is concerned mostly with a retelling.
- Predictions are not realistic to the text.
- Judgments are not supported by text.
- Has difficulty forming questions.

1 point each if student

- Gives off-topic response.
- Is confused.
- Responses are brief and superficial.
- Does not predict.

Chapter 4: Teaching Genre: *Keeping Track of Reading*

Strategy Lesson Plan 6

Teacher Directions: At the beginning of the school year, have students track their reading for seven days. At least once per quarter, have students again track their reading for seven days. Post the results of the class's types of reading, when they read, and total time spent reading. Students' names should not be used.

Name _____   **Week of** _____

Student Directions: Include the date, title of reading material, time spent reading, and total number of pages read. Be sure to include any kind of reading (books, magazines, newspapers, recipes, instructions, game rules, etc.).

Date	Title	Time	Number of Pages

Chapter 4: Teaching Genre: *Small-Group Self-Assessment*

Strategy Lesson Plan 7

Teacher Directions: Periodically have students fill out the following assessment after small group work.

Name _____   Date _____

The most interesting part of our discussion today was _____

_____

_____

_____

My literature study group has improved in _____

_____

My literature study group needs to work on _____

_____

Self-Assessment (4–Excellent, 3–Satisfactory, 2–Could Improve, 1–Unsatisfactory)

1. I read and understood the entire assignment.   _____
2. I responded in my reading notebook.   _____
3. I supported my opinions with evidence from the text.   _____
4. I predicted what might happen next.   _____
5. I asked for clarification when I needed it.   _____
6. I asked questions when I didn't understand.   _____
7. I was able to summarize the most important ideas.   _____
8. I made connections to my life and other texts.   _____
9. I kept eye contact with members of my group.   _____
10. I was a good listener.   _____

                    Total Score   _____

I am improving in _____

My goal is to improve in _____

Chapter 4: Teaching Genre: *Nonfiction*

As adults, most of the reading we do is nonfiction. We read magazines, newspapers, instructions, memos, reports, and so on. Most of our reading is for inquiry. We read for information that is important, useful, and interesting to us. Our students need to be taught the different purposes for reading different genres. They also need to be taught that reading nonfiction requires a different kind of reading than fiction.

The benefits of guiding your students' reading of nonfiction are impressive because:

- Students become more curious and seek to find out more information on subjects that interest them.
- Students deepen their understanding of a topic, and it invites future inquiry.
- Students gain accurate information to support their opinions.
- Students read more critically.
- Students expand their vocabularies.
- Students can connect learning to their lives.
- Students enjoy reading nonfiction.

Most middle-grade and junior high reading programs rely heavily on fiction texts. The first step to improving reading of informational text is to provide more opportunities in the classroom to read, listen to, and discuss nonfiction texts.

What can you do to promote more nonfictional reading?

- Read nonfiction selections aloud.
- Recommend nonfiction books that you have enjoyed.
- Introduce students to great nonfiction authors like Jean Fritz and Kathryn Lasky.
- Read newspapers and magazines to make connections to other learning.

Name: _____   Date: _____

Chapter 4: Teaching Genre: *Recognizing Nonfiction Features*

Strategy Lesson Plan 8

Teacher Directions: Teach students to use the special features of nonfiction to read more critically. Use a science, social studies, math, or language textbook. Have students work in pairs and answer the following questions: (*You may want to have students use more than one text for analysis.*)

What fonts and special text effects give the reader clues that this is important information?

- *Titles*
- *Headings*
- _____
- _____
- _____

What are some verbal cues used in nonfiction text that signal something important?

- *Most important*
- *For example*
- _____
- _____
- _____

Select one illustration or photograph that gives you information to help your understanding of the material. How does it help you?

_____

_____

_____

_____

_____

Name: _____ Date: _____

Chapter 4: *Teaching Genre: Recognizing Nonfiction Features*

Strategy Lesson Plan 8 (continued)

Select one graphic (map, table, graph, cross-section, etc.) that demonstrates important information. What concept does it help you understand?

_____

_____

_____

How would you and your partner use information in the preface or introduction?

_____

_____

_____

Why would you and your partner use the appendix?

_____

_____

_____

Explain the difference between a table of contents and an index.

_____

_____

_____

Explain the difference between an index and a glossary.

_____

_____

_____

Name: _____   Date: _____

Chapter 4: Teaching Genre: *Analyzing the Text Structure of Nonfiction*

Strategy Lesson Plan 9

Teacher Directions: Helping your students to better understand the text structure of informational text empowers them to determine the important information. Provide an array of nonfiction texts at four or five centers. Be sure to include some magazine articles, newspaper articles, textbooks, nonfiction trade books, instructions, manuals, etc. Ask students to work in groups of three or four to find as many examples of each kind of nonfiction structure as they can in a given time period.

Analyzing Text Structure

Name _____   Date _____

Browse through the articles and books at your center. See how many examples you can find of the following nonfiction structures.

Cause and Effect:
Example: Stems and leaves absorb sunlight so the leaves can manufacture food.

Titles in Which Examples Were Found

_____

_____

_____

_____

Compare and Contrast:
Example: Flowering plants are like all other green plants. They use the energy of the sun to manufacture food.

Titles in Which Examples Were Found

_____

_____

_____

_____

Name: _____ Date: _____

Chapter 4: Teaching Genre: *Analyzing the Text Structure of Nonfiction (continued)*

Problem/Solution:

Example: Sunlight cannot reach cells that are underground. For their food, the cells of the plant must rely on the stems and the leaves, which are above ground.

Titles in Which Examples Were Found

_____

_____

_____

_____

Description:

Example: It is this chlorophyll that gives green plants their color.

Titles in Which Examples Were Found

_____

_____

_____

_____

Time/Order:

Example: The growing cycle of a plant can be followed through the following steps:

Titles in Which Examples Were Found

_____

_____

_____

_____

Directions:

Example: When planning a garden, you must prepare the soil for a bountiful crop. There are several things that should be done before planting one seed.

Titles in Which Examples Were Found

_____

_____

_____

_____

Chapter 4: Teaching Genre: *Poetry*

Teaching poetry can make a dramatic difference in enjoying reading and in improving reading comprehension. Poetry is one of the most effective ways to teach students to make universal and emotional connections between what they read and what they know.

Checklist for teaching poetry:

- Teach poems you enjoy.

- Share favorite poets and their poetry.

- Explore poets' lives.

- Read poems aloud to students with passion and joy.

- Read long poems, short poems, funny poems, sad poems, silly poems, animal poems, riddles, love poems, story poems, and so on.

- Have students present poems in an oral interpretation or paired reading.

- Use poems all day long as part of the teaching of all subjects.

- Provide many poetry resources: anthologies, picture book versions, tape recordings, rhyming dictionaries, thesauruses, etc.

- Value all interpretations and responses to poetry.

- Teach students about poems and poetic language to strengthen their poetic power.

- Sing and chant poems aloud together, enjoying the rhythm and rhyme.

Remember:

- Poetry demonstrates language in different forms and patterns.

- Poetry demonstrates figurative language and aids students in the interpretation of complex ideas and images.

- Poetry gives teachers opportunities to read aloud to students.

- Poetry gives opportunities for students to hear certain language that they can later understand in their reading.

- Poetry opens up different backgrounds and cultures.

- Poetry connects us to the past, present, and future.

Chapter 4: Teaching Genre: *The Do's and Don'ts of Teaching Poetry*

Strategy Lesson Plan 10

DO ...

- Choose poetry that you feel is worthwhile.

- Read poems aloud to students often. It may just be a quiet moment for reflection.

- Prepare for reading a poem aloud. The initial reading should be enjoyable.

- Read poetry after activities that activate prior knowledge of the subject of the poem.

- Choose poetry that students can understand.

- Help students recognize the mood of the poem.

- Teach students how to read poems aloud individually or chorally.

- Have students occasionally memorize one of their favorite poems to share with the class.

- Have students share poems they have found outside of school.

- Put students in charge of a poetry center that is updated monthly. This can be determined by theme or poet.

- Encourage students to illustrate poetry ... write about poetry ... dramatize poetry.

- Make poetry a wonderful opportunity for listening.

DON'T ...

- Over-teach by giving a long introduction.

- Make poetry a vocabulary drill.

- Do all the interpreting for your students.

Chapter 4: Teaching Genre: *Connecting Poetry With Other Areas of Study*

Strategy Lesson Plan 11

Teacher Directions: As you and your students are studying any subject area, plan for the inclusion of poetry that may enhance that study.

1. Build prior knowledge with selected lessons in science, social studies, or literature.
2. Predict what the poem will be about.
3. Make connections.
4. Read the poem orally.
5. Make further connections.
6. Clarify anything confusing.
7. Interpret the poet's message.
8. Read silently.

Example

(After studying a unit on weather, introduce the poem, "The Wind Begun To Rock The Grass," by Emily Dickinson.)

Ask students to write down one word or phrase that comes to mind when they think of severe weather. Scribe student responses on a flip chart, overhead, or white board.

thunder	wind
lightning	downed trees
roar of train	broken windows
damage	rainbows
clouds	twisters
floods	Salvation Army
sandbags	injuries

Chapter 4: Teaching Genre: *Connecting Poetry With Other Areas of Study*

Strategy Lesson Plan 11 *(continued)*

Teacher Directions: Read aloud. (It is a good idea for each student to have a copy of the poem.)

The Wind Begun To Rock The Grass
By Emily Dickinson

The wind begun to rock the grass
With threatening tunes and low,
He flung a menace at the earth,
A menace at the sky.

The leaves unhooked themselves from trees
And started all abroad;
The dust did scoop itself like hands
And throw away the road.

The wagons quickened on the streets,
The thunder hurried slow;
The lightning showed a yellow beak,
And then a livid claw.

The birds put up the bars to nests,
The cattle fled to barns;
There came one drop of giant rain,
And then, as if the hands

That held the dams had parted hold,
The waters wrecked the sky,
But overlooked my father's house,
Just quartering a tree.

Chapter 4: Teaching Genre: *Connecting Poetry With Other Areas of Study*

Strategy Lesson Plan 11 (continued)

Example

(After reading the poem, "The Wind Begun To Rock the Grass," by Emily Dickinson, ask students to share another word or phrase that could be used to describe severe weather. Add student responses to the first list on a flip chart, overhead, or white board.)

thunder	**wind**	**"giant rain"**
lightning	**downed trees**	**"menace"**
roar of a train	**broken windows**	**"rock the grass"**
damage	**rainbows**	**"quartering a tree"**
clouds	**twisters**	**"wrecked the sky"**
floods	**Salvation Army**	**fear**
sandbags	**injuries**	**lightning's yellow beak**

Student Directions: Read the poem silently to yourself. As you read the poem, ask yourself these questions:

- How does a storm affect the land?
- How does a storm affect people?
- What images does Emily Dickinson create with her words?
- How does the poem make you feel?
- Can you make any connections to your own experience or knowledge?

Name: _____ Date: _____

Chapter 4: Teaching Genre: *Connecting Poetry With Other Areas of Study*

Strategy Lesson Plan 11 (continued): Interpreting the Author's Message

Summarizing the poem:

Emily Dickinson created several images to describe a violent thunderstorm. In the graphic organizer below, list each of the images created in the poem. Using these images and how they made you feel, write a brief summary.

1. _____

2. _____

3. _____

4. _____

5. _____

6. _____

7. _____

Summary: _____

_____

_____

_____

_____

_____

Chapter 4: Teaching Genre: *What's My Title?*

Strategy Lesson Plan 12

Teacher Directions: This is a great activity for critical thinking and engaging in the reading of poetry. Select six to eight poems that have a similar theme or were written by the same poet. Remove the titles. Students will work in groups of three to four reading one of the poems and deciding what they think the title is.

What's My Title?

Student Directions:

1. Each group selects a "student teacher" who will lead the group discussion.

2. The student teacher reads the poem aloud, selects someone else to read it, or the whole group reads the poem chorally.

3. The student teacher asks if anyone needs anything clarified. The group problem-solves.

4. The student teacher asks each student to read the poem one more time silently, thinking of what the title might be.

5. Once they have had a chance to read the poem, the student teacher leads the group in generating a list of possible titles.

6. For each title, the group will discuss if the title truly fits the poem.

7. The student teacher asks for a volunteer or the entire group will present the poem to the class.

8. The student teacher or someone he/she asks will give the title that the group agreed upon and explain why.

9. The classroom teacher will then give the poem's actual title.

Chapter 4: Teaching Genre: *Myths and Folk Tales*

For the purpose of this text, we will define myths and folk tales as traditional stories and poems that were written as part of man's attempt to understand the natural and spiritual worlds around him. There are numerous other labels that might be attached, such as fantasy, fairy tales, or fables. We will use the terms myths and folk tales.

Myths and folk tales usually began as oral storytelling and were later written down. They were often meant to teach or explain natural phenomenon. They were also entertaining and symbolic of cultural and social mores. These myths and folk tales come from all over the world. Your students encounter them in a variety of ways ... at school, in personal reading, on standardized tests, in movies, and so on.

The narrative structure of a myth or folk tale is very patterned. It is this pattern that can help students comprehend myths and folk tales. Myths and folk tales are meant to tell the listener a story. The setting is merely a staging backdrop for the reader to see the problem played out. Characterization is rather flat. The characters in myths are usually described vividly, but they are not well developed. The characters found in myths and folk tales are very good or very, very bad. They are beautiful or very, very ugly. The plot's suspense and action are the most important components. The problem usually moves swiftly to a quick resolution.

Chapter 4: Teaching Genre: *Motifs in Myths and Folk Tales*

Strategy Lesson Plan 13

Teacher Directions: Students need to know that there are clues that can help them identify certain pieces of literature as myths and folk tales. Teach students the common motifs in myths and folk tales identified by Stith Thompson (1955-1958). Post the motifs in the classroom and/ or give students their own copies.

ANIMALS
Magic
Talking animals
Helpful

TRICKERY
Cleverness
Deception
Wise and unwise

MAGIC
Magical powers
Magical objects
Magical transformations

TESTS
Survival
Truth
Cleverness
Love
Endurance

SUPERNATURAL
Amazing places and things
Creatures with extraordinary powers

Name: _____ Date: _____

Chapter 4: Teaching Genre: *Reading and Writing Myths and Folk Tales*

Strategy Lesson Plan 14

Teacher Directions: As your students read myths and folk tales, they are asked to share their reflections in their reading journals. Students should engage in collaborative analysis of the author's craft and the varied motifs. This analysis can be posted on a wall chart to be added to as more selections are studied. This ongoing discussion can result in students creating their own modern myth or folk tale. Each student can choose a favorite tale and create a new angle or perspective for retelling the story.

Recycled Myths and Folk Tales

Student Directions:

1. Select a familiar or favorite myth or folk tale that you would like to **"recycle."**

    _____

2. Identify the common motifs of the myth or folk tale.

    _____

    _____

3. Create a graphic organizer that outlines the key features of your selected myth.

    Setting:

    Characters and their traits:

Name:_____ Date:_____

Chapter 4: Teaching Genre: *Reading and Writing Myths and Folk Tales (continued)*

Problem:
Event that starts the action:
Next event:
Next event:
Resolution:
Ending:

4. Select one of the following "recycling" ideas to plan your myth or folk tale.
    • Retell the story from the viewpoint of the villain.
    • Use a modern setting for the background of the story.
    • Interweave another myth or folk tale character into the "recycled" format.
    • Revise the story to teach a different lesson.
    • Write a sequel that has a different twist.
    • Retell the story from the viewpoint of one of the minor characters.
    • Write a detailed background of one or more of the characters as a way to explain why the character behaves as he or she does.

Name: _____　Date: _____

Chapter 4: Teaching Genre: *Reading and Writing Myths and Folk Tales (continued)*

5. Create a graphic organizer outlining the plan for your "recycled" myth or folk tale.

Setting:

Characters and their traits:

Problem:

Event that starts the action:

Next event:

Next event:

Resolution:

Ending:

Name:_____ Date:_____

Chapter 4: Teaching Genre: *Reading and Writing Myths and Folk Tales (continued)*

6. Write your recycled myth or folk tale.

Recycled Title

_____

_____

_____

_____

_____

_____

_____

_____

_____

_____

_____

_____

_____

_____

_____

_____

Chapter 5: Assessing Reading Comprehension: *Introduction*

Assessment should drive instruction. Unfortunately, assessment and grades are often viewed in the same way. For the purposes of this chapter, we will analyze three ways to assess reading comprehension: retelling, taking standardized tests, and essay response. The major reason to assess is to inform our teaching; however, the reality is that teachers must give grades in most schools. The question becomes how and when we can use assessment to determine a grade.

First, it is important to know why we assess.

- Assessment helps you set concrete standards for what students should know and be able to do.
- Assessment helps you strategically plan what to teach.
- Assessment helps you strategically plan when to teach a particular skill, concept, or strategy.
- Assessment tells you whether or not your students are accomplishing the standards you have set.
- Assessment helps you to demonstrate growth to students, parents, and administration.
- Assessment helps you to evaluate materials, programs, and learning opportunities in the classroom.
- Assessment makes you a more effective teacher.

Authentic assessment also helps students.

- Assessment helps students to set their own learning goals.
- Assessment helps students understand how their grades are determined and how they can improve upon their performance.
- Assessment helps students evaluate their own work.

That is why teachers must share with each student the information that the assessment gives them. Informing students of individual grades does not teach students anything. Grades literally hold no value to the learning process without understanding the standards for the assessment and the results of the assessment.

Assessment = HELP

Chapter 5: Informal Reading Inventories: *Establishing Big Goals With Specific Standards*

In most states, the learning goals and standards have been set by state boards of education. In Illinois, the State Goals 1, 2, 3, and 5 apply to reading achievement. As classroom teachers, we can use these goals and standards to clarify our own assessment standards. The key lies in the quality of the questions that we ask.

Example

State Goal #1: Students will be able to read with understanding and fluency.

Broad Question: Are my students able to read with understanding and fluency?

Assessment Question: How do I know?

Specific Assessment Questions:

- Are my students able to read with understanding by making connections to their own lives? How do I know?
- Are my students able to read with understanding by making connections to the world? How do I know?
- Are my students able to read with understanding by making connections to other texts they have read? How do I know?
- Are my students able to read with understanding and fluency by using effective word analysis? How do I know?
- Are my students able to read with understanding by making predictions? How do I know?
- Are my students able to read with understanding by making inferences? How do I know?
- Are my students able to read with understanding by asking questions? How do I know?
- Are my students able to read with understanding by clarifying what they do not understand? How do I know?
- Are my students able to read with understanding by visualizing as they read? How do I know?
- Are my students able to read informational texts with understanding? How do I know?
- Are my students able to locate, organize, and use information from texts that they are reading? How do I know?

These are the kinds of questions that will guide teachers to meaningful and authentic assessment.

Chapter 5: Informal Reading Inventories: *How Do I Know?*

Teacher Directions: Provide a variety of avenues that a student may access to demonstrate what he or she knows and is able to do. From these performances, select those that will be your evidence for reading comprehension.

FORMAL ASSESSMENT

1. Tests and quizzes
2. Essays and reports
3. Written projects
4. Prepared presentations
5. Standardized tests

INFORMAL ASSESSMENT

1. Classroom discussions
2. Literature circles and discussion roles
3. Teacher/student conferences
4. Quick writes
5. Reading log (journal)
6. Surveys
7. Portfolio
8. Artistic responses
9. Anecdotal notes

*** *Talk routinely to students about why they are reading this text and how they should be thinking as they read the text.*

MODEL, MODEL, MODEL!

Students need to know what reading successfully feels like, looks like, and sounds like.

Chapter 5: Retelling: *Types of Retelling*

Retelling can be one of the best ways to assess and monitor reading comprehension over time. It is an authentic, natural assessment that occurs as part of classroom learning. To retell, students must reflect on what they have read and organize and determine the most important information. Students must determine key events, characters, problems, settings, and resolutions.

Teacher Directions: Remind students that retelling is an important part of their reading as well as their communication in everyday life. Think about how often we retell the plot of a movie or a school event.

NARRATIVE RETELLING

- Author/title

- Main characters

- Minor characters

- Main events (plot)

- Setting (time and place)

- Problems

- Solutions

- Theme

INFORMATIONAL TEXT RETELLING

Basic components of informational text retelling:

- Topic

- Author's purpose

- Most important ideas

- Information in graphs, charts, pictures

- Specialized vocabulary

- Listing of what you learned

Chapter 5: Retelling: *Steps to Teaching Retelling*

Teacher Directions: Use the following steps to teach retelling skills to students.

STEPS TO TEACHING RETELLING

- Explicitly explain to students how to do a retell. A big mistake is to assume that students know how to retell.

- Explain to students the difference between a retelling and a summary. *(They serve two different purposes.)*

- Explain to students why they need to know how to retell.

- Model retelling. Think aloud. Tell students how you determined what you would include in your retelling.

- Teach students to use a graphic organizer to plan their retelling.

- Ask students to retell shorter selections first before they retell longer texts.

- Have students practice retelling as part of their reading log or journal.

- Develop a retelling rubric with your students.

- Have students assess one of their own retellings with the rubric.

- Have students assess a partner's retelling using the rubric.

Chapter 5: Retelling: *Retelling Rubric*

Retelling Rubric

4 points each if
- <u>Main event(s)</u>: Retells events in order with some detail. Makes connections to self, world, and/or other texts.
- <u>Characters</u>: Identifies all main characters. Makes some inferences about characters' personality traits and motivations.
- <u>Setting</u>: Includes specific setting information (if available).
- <u>Problem</u>: Identifies problems and/or solutions with some analysis and/or prediction.
- <u>Theme</u>: Demonstrates understanding of author's theme using inferencing and personal connections.

3 points each if
- <u>Main event(s)</u>: Retells events with a beginning, middle, and end.
- <u>Characters</u>: Identifies all main characters.
- <u>Setting</u>: Includes setting information (if available).
- <u>Problem</u>: Identifies problems and/or solutions.
- <u>Theme</u>: Can predict something of significance will occur.

2 points each if
- <u>Main event(s)</u>: Identifies at least one key event.
- <u>Characters</u>: Identifies some main characters.
- <u>Setting</u>: May or may not know time or place.
- <u>Problem</u>: May or may not identify a problem.
- Retelling is insufficient.

1 point each if
- <u>Main event(s)</u>: Limited understanding of what is happening in the story.
- <u>Characters</u>: Can name one or two characters.
- <u>Setting</u>: Does not know.
- <u>Problem</u>: Limited or missing.
- Retelling is confusing.

0 points each if
- No effort is made.

Chapter 5: Informal Reading Inventories: *Retelling Checklist*

Student _____ Date _____

Title _____ Pages _____

SCORE GUIDE: 1 (Insufficient)   2 (Minimal)   3 (Adequate)   4 (Excellent)
N/A (Not applicable to this reading)

_____ 1. Gives author and title.

_____ 2. Provides information about major and minor characters.

_____ 3. Makes inferences.

_____ 4. Describes the setting.

_____ 5. Identifies problem(s) and/or solution(s).

_____ 6. Makes personal connections to the reading.

_____ 7. Identifies the theme.

_____ 8. Makes a prediction.

_____ 9. Generates an evaluation or question about the reading.

_____ 10. Demonstrated effective word analysis.

SCORE: _____

Teacher Comments: _____

_____

_____

_____

_____

Chapter 5: Informal Reading Inventories: *Self-Assessment of Retelling*

Student _____ Date _____

Title _____ Pages _____

I included the following in my retelling:

- Author/title _____

- Main characters _____

- Minor characters _____

- Main events (plot) _____

- Setting (time and place) _____

- Problems _____

- Solutions _____

- Theme _____

Strategies I used when I read:

- I made personal connections. _____

- I made predictions. _____

- I asked "On My Own" questions. _____

- I used fix-up strategies as I read. _____

- I could summarize the most important parts of the reading when I finished. _____

My goal for improving my reading is _____

_____

_____

Chapter 5: Standardized Tests: *Introduction*

All of the reading strategies discussed in this book will enable students to perform well when taking standardized tests. Teachers must teach students the connection between using these strategies for their everyday reading and the reading they must do to answer standardized multiple-choice questions.

The reading passages and the questions that follow in a standardized reading test reflect two types of reading:

Reading for Literary Experience: These reading passages will be short story selections and passages from novels, poetry, myths, and plays.

Reading to Gain Information: These reading passages will be nonfiction from magazines, scientific and social trade journals, and newspapers.

106

Chapter 5: Putting It All Together: *Standards for Reading Questions*

The Illinois Standards Achievement Test for Reading has five reading standards. Understanding these standards will guide teachers as they plan authentic assessment of reading that matches the expectations on the standardized tests that students must take. The teacher can use the following standards to plan practice assessments with any material used as a part of classroom instruction.

1. **Comprehension of Literary Works:** All questions in this category evaluate student understanding of any kind of literary text. The implication for our teaching is to provide students with a variety of genres and the strategies to comprehend different kinds of text.

2. **Comprehension of Informational Text:** All questions in this category evaluate student understanding of information text. The implication for our teaching is to provide students with a balance of nonfiction and fiction reading and the strategies to comprehend both kinds of text.

3. **Application of Reading Strategies–Identifying Main Ideas:** All questions in this category evaluate whether or not a student can identify the main ideas from a text. The implication for our teaching is explicitly to teach students *how to identify main ideas in a variety of genres.*

4. **Application of Reading Strategies–Making Inferences:** All questions in this category evaluate whether or not a student can analyze main ideas in a text and draw conclusions from that information. The implication for our teaching is explicitly to teach students *how to make inferences when they read a variety of texts.*

5. **Vocabulary Questions:** All questions in this category evaluate how students use word attack skills to understand important words and concepts. The implication for our teaching is explicitly to teach students *how to use word attack and context clues to figure out words and concepts they do not know.*

Name: _____ Date: _____

Chapter 5: Putting It All Together: *Practicing for Standardized Tests*

Strategy Lesson Plan 1

Teacher Directions: Although there are many published practice samples of reading tests, the teacher's best opportunities to have students practice for standardized tests will come from the reading being done as part of classroom instruction. The following is a sample of some biographical information on Emily Dickinson. If I were going to do an author study on eccentric poets, I might select some of Emily Dickinson's poems for literature study. One of my activities for reading assessment would be to have students read the following information on Emily Dickinson and answer some multiple-choice questions.

Emily Dickinson

Perhaps one of the most eccentric writers of all time may be Emily Dickinson. She is considered to be one of the greatest American poets. She is famous for over 1800 poems, most of which were published after her death in 1886.

She was born Elizabeth Dickinson on December 10, 1830, in Amherst, Massachusetts. Emily, Austin, her older brother, and her younger sister, Lavinia, were nurtured in a quiet, reserved family headed by their authoritative father, Edward Dickinson, a well-to-do lawyer. Throughout Emily's life, she had a minimal relationship with her mother. This may have influenced her solitary lifestyle. The Dickinson children were raised in the Christian tradition, and they were expected to follow their father's religious beliefs and values without argument.

It was the tradition of the time for daughters to remain at home and help with the housework until they were married. But Emily never married. For Emily, "her friends and companions" were the books that filled her room. She was shy and demure. Whenever the doorbell would ring, she would run upstairs to avoid seeing anyone. As she did her household chores, Emily would write down poetry in the margins of the newspaper or on scraps of grocery paper. She would take these bits and pieces of verse to her room where she would make clean copies of them. She would then place the poems in a locked box in her bureau. Emily loved the seclusion of her room.

As the daughter of a prominent politician, Emily had the benefit of a good education and attended the Amherst Academy. Although she was successful in college, Emily returned after only one year at the academy to Amherst where she began her life of seclusion.

Name: _____ Date: _____

Chapter 5: Putting It All Together: *Practicing for Standardized Tests (cont.)*

Strategy Lesson Plan 1 (continued)

Although Emily never married, she did have significant relationships with a select few. It was during this period, following her return from school, that Emily began to dress all in white. She chose only a few people with whom to correspond. Emily seldom left her father's house. In fact, she left Amherst only a dozen times, usually to go to Boston to have an eye problem treated. Emily had no extended exposure to the world outside her Amherst education. During this time in her early twenties, Emily began to write poetry seriously. Fortunately, during those rare journeys, Emily met two very influential men who would be sources of inspiration and guidance: Charles Wadsworth and Thomas Wentworth Higginson.

In her seclusion, Emily continued to write poetry. As a result of the advent of the Civil War and the death of her father, Dickinson's poetry changed. In this most productive period of her lifetime, Emily wrote over 800 poems.

The later years of Dickinson's life were primarily spent in mourning and continued seclusion. When she became ill, she allowed the doctor only to ask her questions from the adjoining room. She was 55 when she died of a kidney disease. On May 15, 1886, Emily died. The world lost one of its most talented and powerful poets. After Emily's death, her sister, Lavinia, found her poems and made it her life's goal to get them published.

Eventually her poetry was published. The poems were grouped into classes—Friends, Nature, Love, and Death. When the poems were first published, editors arranged her works with titles, rearranged syntax, and standardized Dickinson's grammar. Fortunately in 1955, Thomas Johnson published Dickinson's poems in their original form, and the world could then celebrate the creative genius of Emily Dickinson.

Name: _____ Date: _____

Chapter 5: Putting It All Together: *Practicing for Standardized Tests—Multiple-Choice Questions (cont.)*

Strategy Lesson Plan 1 (continued)

Student Directions: Answer the following questions about Emily Dickinson. Circle the correct answer.

1. Who were Emily's "friends and companions" as she grew up?
   a.   Austin and Lavinia
   b.   The neighborhood children
   c.   Her books
   d.   Wadsworth and Higginson

2. What is this article mostly about?
   a.   Emily's controlling father
   b.   The Civil War
   c.   Emily Dickinson's poetry
   d.   Emily Dickinson's eccentric life

3. What does the word ECCENTRIC mean?
   a.   Odd or strange
   b.   Creative
   c.   Shy
   d.   Hysterical

4. All of the following illustrate Dickinson's eccentricity *except ...*
   a.   Dressing only in white
   b.   Running upstairs when the doorbell rang
   c.   Not allowing the doctor to examine her
   d.   Writing poetry

5. Why do you think Emily didn't try to get her poems published when she was alive?
   a.   She did not know how to get them published.
   b.   She didn't want to draw any attention to herself.
   c.   Her father wouldn't let her.
   d.   She didn't think she would get paid for them.

110

Name: _____ Date: _____

Chapter 5: Putting It All Together: *Open Essay Response*

Many standardized reading tests include a written response component. Teaching students to make connections to their own lives and the world is a critical skill that students need in order to write successfully to these prompts.

Recommendations:

- Teach students the standards for a quality written response.
- Provide students with the reading response rubric.
- Routinely ask students to respond to their reading in writing. Ask students to self-assess using the reading response rubric.
- Provide five explicit prompts for students to respond to in their reading logs (journals).
- Give a "Quick Write" assessment. Have students write to a specific prompt within a given period of time. Assess with the reading response rubric.

Example

Student Directions: Answer the following question on the lines below.

What can we learn from Emily Dickinson's life and poetry? Use information from the story and your own observations and conclusions to answer the question. Use your own paper if you need more room.

_____

_____

_____

_____

_____

_____

_____

_____

_____

_____

Chapter 5: Putting It All Together: *Open Essay Response* (cont.)

Reading Response Rubric

4 points each if the student

- Understands and identifies main ideas in the text.
- Effectively interprets and makes connections to other parts of the text and to own ideas.
- Gives specific examples from text to support answer.
- Makes relevant connections to prior knowledge.

3 points each if the student

- Identifies some key information in text.
- Interprets and makes connections to text and to own ideas. May have some gaps.
- Gives examples from text to support answer. Some may be general.
- Attempts to make connections to prior knowledge.

2 points each if the student

- Shows limited understanding of the main information in the text.
- Gives simplistic interpretation of text.
- Gives limited support from text information.
- Makes generalizations without clear connection to text.

1 point each if the student

- Shows limited understanding; may give inaccurate information.
- Makes little or no attempt to interpret the text.
- Gives no support from text.
- Makes no connection to prior knowledge.

0 points each if the student

- Does not address the prompt.
- Gives insufficient information.

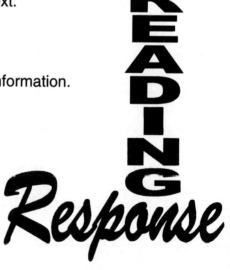

Appendix

Name: _____   Date: _____

Keeping a Writer's Notebook

Student Directions: Record what you write and the reasons you write in your writer's notebook.

What I Write	
What I Write for Myself and Others	**What I Write for My Teacher(s)**

Name: _____ Date: _____

Using Predictions to Make Connections

Making a Prediction

Student Directions: As you read, pay close attention to the parts of the text when you find yourself making **a prediction**. Using the form below, jot down the first and last word of the passage or identify the picture that helped you make a prediction. Then write down your prediction. When you have finished your reading, go back and check to see if your predictions actually happened. Then write down what really happened.

Passage or Picture: _____

Prediction: _____

_____

Was your prediction right? _____ If not, what did happen? _____

_____

Passage or Picture: _____

Prediction: _____

_____

Was your prediction right? _____ If not, what did happen? _____

_____

Passage or Picture: _____

Prediction: _____

_____

Was your prediction right? _____ If not, what did happen? _____

_____

Passage or Picture: _____

Prediction: _____

_____

Was your prediction right? _____ If not, what did happen? _____

_____

Name: _____ Date: _____

Making Connections to Your Own Life

Student Directions: As you read, pay close attention to the parts of the text when you find yourself making **a connection to your own life**. Using the form below, jot down the first and last word of the passage or identify the picture where you made the connection to your life. Then write down your connection.

Passage or Picture: _____

_____

Connection to My Life: _____

_____

_____

_____

_____

_____

Passage or Picture: _____

_____

Connection to My Life: _____

_____

_____

_____

_____

Name: _____ Date: _____

Making Connections to Another Text

Student Directions: As you read, pay close attention to the parts of the text when you find yourself making **a connection to another text that you have read**. Using the form below, jot down the first and last word of the passage or identify the picture where you made the connection to another text. Then write down your connection.

Passage or Picture: _____

_____

Connection to Another Text I've Read: _____

_____

_____

_____

_____

_____

Passage or Picture: _____

_____

Connection to Another Text I've Read: _____

_____

_____

_____

_____

_____

Name: _____ Date: _____

Making Connections to the World

Student Directions: As you read, pay close attention to the parts of the text when you find yourself making **a connection to other knowledge you have about the world.** Using the form below, jot down the first and last word of the passage or identify the picture where you made the connection to other knowledge. Then write down your connection.

Passage or Picture: _____

_____

Connection to the World: _____

_____

_____

_____

_____

_____

Passage or Picture: _____

_____

Connection to the World: _____

_____

_____

_____

_____

_____

Name: _____ Date: _____

Determining the Most Important Ideas and Themes

Student Directions: As you read, record the main ideas and themes in the selection.

Mapping Main Ideas As You Read		
Page #	**One Main Idea**	**One or Two Details**

Name: _____ Date: _____

Activating Prior Knowledge

DO YOU KNOW THESE WORDS?

If you think you know or you are sure of the meaning, please write your definition in the appropriate column.

1. _____

2. _____

3. _____

No clue	I've seen it or heard it	I think I know	Yes, I've got it
1.	1.	1.	1.
2.	2.	2.	2.
3.	3.	3.	3.

Name: _____ Date: _____

Word-Context-Connection

Student Directions: Identify one word from your reading that you do not know. Then complete the graphic organizer below about the word.

Context-Connection

Write the word in context: _____

_____

- **Circle the word needing clarifying.**

- **Read the surrounding sentences.**

Identify two possible definitions:

    1. _____

    2. _____

Look up the definition in the dictionary:

_____

_____

Use the word in a different context:

_____

_____

_____

Make a personal connection:

_____

_____

_____

_____

Name: _____ Date: _____

Idiomatic Interpretation

FUN WITH IDIOMS

High-frequency Word: _____

Idiomatic Expressions: *(To be generated by students and teacher.)*

1. _____

2. _____

3. _____

4. _____

5. _____

Student Directions: Use each of the idioms in sentences that clearly reflect each idiomatic expression.

1. _____

_____

2. _____

_____

3. _____

_____

4. _____

_____

5. _____

_____

Answer Keys

P. 22   Chapter 1: Questioning: Teacher Model/ Guided Student Practice
Teacher Model:
1. Right There
2. Think and Search
3. Author and You
4. On My Own
Guided Student Practice: Answers will vary.

P. 62   Chapter 3: Teaching Vocabulary: "Family Matters"
Answer will vary. Possible answers are given.
Protect: protection, protective, protector, protectable, protectorate, protectory, protectorship, protectionism, protected, protects
Community: communities, commune, communal, communalism, communistic
Motion: motions, motioned, motioning, motional, motionless, motionlessly
Wood: woods, wooded, woody, woodwork, woodcut, wooden, woodland, woodcraft, woodsman
Imagine: image, imagined, imagining, imagination, imaginative, imaginary, imagery, imaginable
Original: origin, originality, originally, originate, originated, origination

P. 72   Chapter 4: Teaching Genre: Literary Elements of Realistic Fiction, Strategy Lesson Plan 2
Answers will vary, but should include these basic ideas.
1. Introduction: the beginning part of a reading selection that explains and leads into the main part of the text
2. Setting: where the story takes place; the time and location
3. Major Characters: the people or characters around whom most of the action or conflict of the story revolves
4. Minor Characters: the people or characters in the story that are not essential to that story
5. Conflict: the problem or struggle that the main characters must resolve in the story
6. Point of View: who is telling the story; from whose perspective we are seeing the action
7. Plot: what happens in the story; the events of the story
8. Theme: the recurring, unifying subject or idea of the story; the message the author is trying to convey
9. Resolution: the part of the story where the plot is made clear and the problem is solved
10. Imagery: the use of descriptive language and figures of speech to allow the reader to see in his or her mind's eye what is occurring in the story

P. 73 Strategy Lesson Plan 2 (cont.)
Answers will vary, but should include these basic ideas.
1. Analogy: showing the logical relationships between pairs of words
2. Alliteration: the repetition of a consonant sound at the beginning of a series of words
3. Atmosphere: the general tone or mood of a piece of writing
4. Inference: a conclusion or opinion arrived at by reasoning or assumption
5. Foreshadowing: the indication or suggestion of something to come given early in a piece of writing
6. Mood: the predominant feeling or tone of a piece
7. Simile: a comparison between two things that are not necessarily similar by using the word *like* or *as*
8. Metaphor: a comparison that implies a relationship by saying that one things *is* another
9. Symbolism: using an object, event, or creature to stand for a universal idea or quality
10. Irony: when the opposite of what is expected occurs

P. 90   Chapter 4: Teaching Genre: Connecting Poetry With Other Areas of Study, Strategy Lesson Plan 11
Answers may vary. Choose seven of these:
1. wind begun to rock the grass
2. flung a menace at the earth
3. leaves unhooked themselves from trees
4. dust did scoop itself like hands And throw away the road
5. thunder hurried slow
6. lightening showed a yellow beak, And then a livid claw
7. birds put up the bars to nests
8. giant rain
9. hands That held the dams had parted hold
10. waters wrecked the sky
11. quartering a tree

P. 110   Chapter 5: Putting It All Together: Practicing for Standardized Tests—Multiple-Choice Questions
1. c
2. d
3. a
4. d
5. b

P. 110   Chapter 5: Putting It All Together: Open Essay Response
Answers will vary. Teacher check answers.

Bibliography

Allen, Janet. 1995. *It's Never Too Late: Leading Adolescents to Lifelong Literacy.* Portsmouth, NH: Heinemann.

Allen, Janet and Kyle Gonzales. 1998. *There's Room for Me Here: Literacy Workshop in the Middle Schools.* York, ME; Stenhouse.

Allington, Richard. 1997. In *Building a Knowledge Base in Readings,* eds. Jane Braunger and Jan Lewis. Newark, DE: International Reading Association.

Atwell, Nancie. 1998. *In the Middle: New Understandings About Writing, Reading, and Learning.* Portsmouth, NH: Heinemann.

Burke, Jim. 1999. *I Hear America Reading: Why We Read - What We Read.* Portsmouth, NH: Heinemann.

Burke, Jim. 1999. *The English Teacher's Companion: A Complete Guide to Classroom, Curriculum, and the Profession.* Portsmouth, NH: Heinemann.

Calkins, Lucy. 1986. *The Art of Teaching Writing.* Portsmouth, NH: Heinemann.

Culhan, Ruth. 1998. *Picture Books: An Annotated Bibliography.* Portland, OR: Northwest Regional Educational Laboratory.

Cunningham, Patricia and Richard Allington. 1999. *Classrooms That Work: They Can All Read and Write.* NY: Longman.

Daniels, Harvey. 1994. *Literature Circles: Voice and Choice in the Classroom.* York, ME: Stenhouse.

Fletcher, Ralph and Jean Portalupi. 1998. *Craft Lessons: Teaching Writing K–8.* York, ME: Stenhouse.

Fountas, Irene and Gay Sue Pinnell. 1996. *Guided Reading: Good First Teaching for All Children.* Portsmouth, NH. Heinemann.

Harvey, Stephanie. 1998. *Nonfiction Matters: Reading, Writing and Research in Grades 3–8.* York, ME: Stenhouse.

Johnson, Janet. 1998. *Content Area Reading.* NY: Delmar.

Keene, Ellin and Susan Zimmerman. 1997. *Mosaic of Thought: Teaching Comprehension in a Reader's Workshop.* Portsmouth, NH: Heinemann.

Lane, Barry. 1993. *After the End: Teaching and Learning Creative Revision.* Portsmouth, NH: Heinemann.

Opitz, M. and T. Rasinski. 1999. *Good-Bye Round Robin.* Portsmouth, NH: Heinemann.

Pearson, P.D. and B. Taylor. 1999. *Schools That Beat the Odds.*

Pearson, P.D. and L. Fielding. 1991. "Comprehension Instruction." ed. R. Barr, M. Kamil, P. Mosenthan, and P.D. Pearson. *Handbook of Reading Research,* Vol. 2, pp 815–860. NY: Longman.

Robinson, Linda. 1998. "Understanding Middle School Students." In *Into Focus: Understanding and Creating Middle School Readers,* ed. Kylene Beers and Barbara G. Samuels. Norwood, MA: Christopher-Gordon.

Routman, Regie. 2000. *Conversations: Strategies for Teaching, Learning, and Evaluating.* Portsmouth, NH: Heinemann.

Weaver, Constance. 1998. *Practicing What We Know: Informed Reading Instruction.* Urbana, IL: National Council of Teachers of English.

Weaver, Constance. 1998. *Reconsidering a Balanced Approach to Reading.* Urbana, IL: National Council of Teachers of English.